THIS PAGE LEFT BLANK...

DISCLAIMER

The information given in the book has been prepared by the Author. The Author requests it be acknowledged as the source of this information. The author believe that all information contained in this book is accurate; however, the user should be aware that the recommendations provided in this book do not replace any standard or regulation.

Although the author have made every effort to ensure that the information in this book was correct at press time, the author do not assume and hereby disclaim any liability to any party for any loss, damage, or disruption caused by errors or omissions, whether such errors or omissions result from negligence, accident, or any other cause.

All images are copyrighted to their respective owners.

Author
Kamran Ahmad

ABOUT THIS BOOK

This book has been designed for the information and knowledge of all those who want to know about daily workplace fire hazards and how to control and manage them.

The book deals with fire safety topics like fire behavior, fire triangle, fire tetrahedron, fire classes, fire stages, fire control theory, fire special hazards, workplace practices, fire extinguishment, sprinkler systems, fire detection & alarm systems, building evacuation and fire program management etc.

Each topic is then spread out so that reader know the basics about the topic at first and then gradually proceed to know the factors and sub topics that constitute it and lastly how to eliminate or control them through different control measures available in a given scenario.

The control measures given has been kept to generic solutions in a typical scenario. Specific standards references have been intentionally avoided as the book is for general purposes and not serving a typical country standards.

Having said that some standards despite being of a particular country is considered universal and is accepted as such like in the case of fire classes and how the method of P.A.S.S. etc.

While every effort has been made to ensure the accuracy of the contents, the book is intended only as a training aid and does not intend to approve or disapprove any specific product, service, or practice.

Every effort has been made to ensure given information has been accurate and precise. But in case of errors please notify so as to be excluded in future editions.

This page left blank…

TABLE OF CONTENTS

Introduction

The safety professional bears a significant responsibility in safeguarding the workplace against fires. Their primary objective is to ensure that the property is adequately protected to prevent severe financial losses for the organization. Moreover, they have a moral obligation to protect employees and the community at large from the devastating impact of fires.

Industrial fire protection and prevention entail identifying potential fire hazards, assessing the likelihood of unwanted fire incidents, and implementing control measures to mitigate these risks to an acceptable level. These controls can take the form of engineering strategies, administrative measures, or a combination thereof, depending on the specific circumstances. Additionally, emergency response is an integral part of fire protection and prevention, involving the organization, training, and coordination of competent employees to effectively handle emergencies such as fires, accidents, or other disasters.

FIRE PREVENTION VERSUS FIRE PROTECTION

Fire prevention and fire protection are two distinct concepts that safety professionals must distinguish. Fire prevention involves eliminating or reducing the possibility of a fire starting. For a fire to start, it needs a heat source, a fuel source, and an initiator. Fire prevention programs can address these elements by managing the heat and fuel sources and preventing behaviors that can bring them together. In the workplace, programs like housekeeping and inspection can help prevent fires.

Effective fire prevention requires vigilance, action, and cooperation. Vigilance involves regular workplace inspections to identify fire hazards. Action includes correcting hazardous situations, such as cleaning up debris, installing effective storage and ventilation systems, establishing work rules and maintenance policies, and repairing or replacing faulty equipment or electrical systems. Cooperation between employers and employees is essential to ensure everyone understands their common interest in fire prevention and works together to eliminate fire hazards.

Fire protection engineers use engineering and scientific principles to protect people, property, and operations from fires and explosions. Their work includes evaluating buildings for fire risks, designing fire detection and suppression systems, and researching materials and consumer products to reduce fire hazards.

Safety professionals recognize that fire prevention cannot be 100% successful, and it is essential to plan for and mitigate damage if a fire does occur. Fire protection strategies aim to minimize the extent of the fire, including reducing fire hazards through inspections, facility and process layouts, and designing fire detection and suppression systems. Workplace fire safety planning should include provisions for fire suppression or extinguishment and the evacuation of people in the event of a fire emergency. Fire-extinguishing systems include sprinklers, fire doors and walls, portable extinguishers, and standpipe hose systems. Evacuation planning should consider egress, detection and notification systems, and emergency preparedness.

Fire protection involves the creation of a comprehensive system that combines various design features and systems to work together and provide backup in case of failure. According to the National Fire Protection Association (NFPA), fire protection encompasses six opportunities to intervene against a fire, arranged based on the potential growth of fire severity over time:

- Prevent the occurrence of fire altogether.
- Slow down the initial growth of the fire.
- Detect the fire at an early stage, allowing for effective intervention before it becomes severe.
- Implement automatic or manual suppression systems to extinguish the fire.
- Design spaces that can confine the fire.
- Safely evacuate the occupants to a secure location.

Fire protection includes the utilization of both active systems like automatic detection systems and passive fire-protection systems that prevent the spread of fire and smoke. It's evident that the activities aimed at fire prevention differ from those focused on minimizing the impact of a fire once it has occurred. Therefore, an effective fire-safety program necessitates incorporating both prevention and protection measures.

Fire Behavior

SCIENCE

Understanding the science of fire is crucial for comprehending its behavior and taking appropriate fire safety measures. While you may have a basic understanding of fire, heat, and temperature, it is important to delve into these concepts from a more scientific standpoint. Fire can manifest in various forms, but they all involve a chemical reaction that produces heat when a fuel source interacts with oxygen or a similar substance. When combustion occurs, heat is generated at a rate that exceeds its dissipation, leading to a substantial increase in temperature.

PHYSICAL AND CHEMICAL CHANGES OF MATTER

When observing the world around us, we encounter various materials collectively referred to as matter. Matter is considered the substance that comprises our universe, occupying space and possessing mass. Matter can undergo different types of changes, both physical and chemical, in relation to fire.

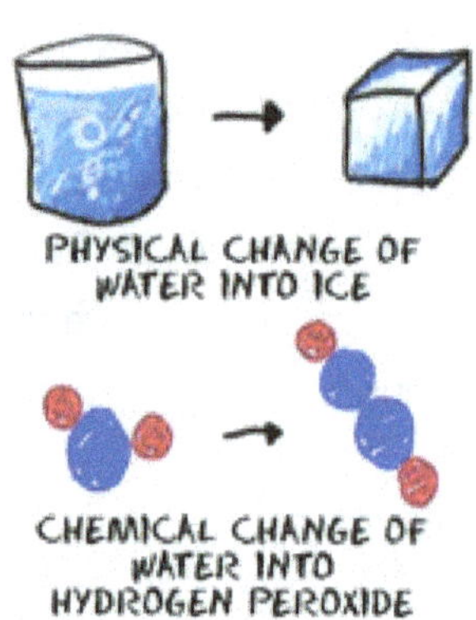

A physical change refers to a transformation where a substance remains chemically unchanged but alters in terms of size, shape, or appearance. Examples of physical changes include water freezing, transitioning from a liquid to a solid state, or boiling, transitioning from a liquid to a gaseous state.

On the other hand, a chemical change occurs when a substance transforms from one type of matter into another. Such changes often involve the reaction of two or more substances to form different compounds. One example of a chemical reaction is oxidation, which involves the combination of oxygen (or similar substances) with other materials. Oxidation processes can occur slowly, such as the combination of oxygen with iron to produce rust, or rapidly, as in the combustion of methane (natural gas). Given that oxygen is a prevalent element on Earth (composing 21 percent of our atmosphere), it readily reacts with many other elements found on the planet.

Both physical and chemical changes typically involve the exchange of energy. The potential energy of a fuel is released during combustion and transformed into kinetic energy. Reactions that release energy as they occur are referred to as exothermic. Fire, as an exothermic chemical reaction called combustion, releases energy in the form of heat and sometimes light. Conversely, reactions that absorb energy as they proceed are called endothermic. For instance, converting water from a liquid to a gaseous state (steam) requires the input of energy and is an endothermic physical reaction. In subsequent sections, you will learn how the conversion of water to steam plays a significant role in controlling and extinguishing fires.

DIFFERENT MODES OF COMBUSTION

Combustion is a rapid and self-sustaining chemical process that generates heat and often light. Fire itself is a form of combustion. Modes of combustion can be distinguished based on where the chemical reaction takes place.

In flaming combustion, the oxidation process involves fuel in the gas phase. This requires converting liquid or solid fuels into the gas phase or vaporizing them. When heated, both liquid and solid fuels release vapors that mix with oxygen and can burn, resulting in the production of flames. Some solid fuels, especially porous ones that can char, can undergo surface oxidation without producing flames. This non-flaming combustion is known as smoldering. Examples of non-flaming combustion include burning charcoal or smoldering fabric and upholstery.

Combustion can be further defined as an exothermic chemical reaction between a substance and oxygen. It involves chain reactions that include free hydrogen atoms (H2), hydroxyl free radicals (OH), and free oxygen molecules (O2). The combination of hydrogen and oxygen forms water molecules, which in turn can react to produce more water and more hydrogen molecules. This chemical chain reaction continues until all the fuel is consumed by the fire.

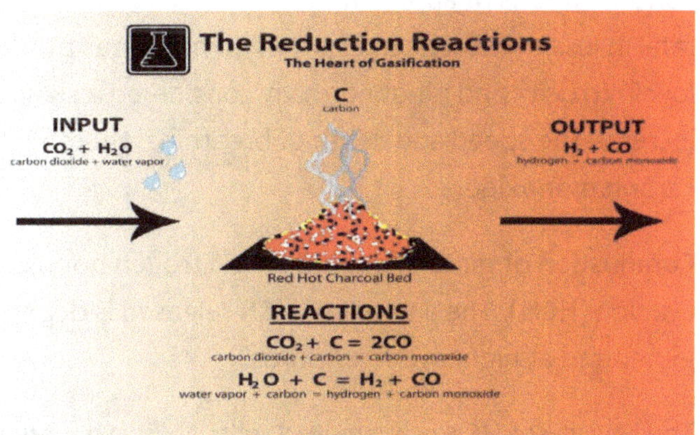

To fully grasp combustion, understanding oxidation is essential. Oxidation refers to the chemical combination of a substance with an oxidizer. With combustion, the energy accompanying oxidation is commonly released as heat and light. The speed at which oxidation occurs can vary, ranging from slow processes like rusting iron and yellowing paper to the rapid nature of combustion. The crucial difference between slow oxidation and combustion is that combustion proceeds so quickly that heat is generated at a rate faster than it can be dissipated, leading to a significant temperature increase in the substance.

The rates of combustion for gases, liquids, and solids depend on several factors. For solids, the combustion rate is primarily influenced by the size of the solid particles, with smaller particles burning at a higher rate. The rate of combustion for flammable liquids varies depending on whether it occurs in a still pool, flowing current, or as a spray or foam. Flammable gases' combustion rate depends on the extent to which the gas mixes with air before combustion and the level of motion and turbulence of the gases.

During combustion, four major products are produced: heat, smoke, light, and fire gases. These products are crucial considerations for fire-related purposes, not only for extinguishing fires but also for ensuring life safety and designing buildings. The primary cause of death in a fire is often attributed to the toxic fire gases.

Heat, as a product of combustion, plays a significant role in spreading the fire by preheating adjacent fuels and making them more prone to ignition. Insufficient protection from heat can result in burns, damage to the respiratory tract, dehydration, and heat exhaustion.

The second product of combustion is smoke, which consists of airborne solid and liquid particulates and fire gases produced during the process. Smoke is a major contributor to fire-related fatalities, accounting for 50 to 75 percent of deaths. Smoke reduces visibility, irritates the eyes and lungs, and often carries lethal fire gases.

The type and quantity of fire gases generated during combustion depend on the chemical composition of the burning material, the availability of oxygen, the temperature, and the potential interactions between particles and gases. The effects of these fire gases on the body are influenced by their concentration, the duration of exposure, and the physical condition of the individual. Carbon monoxide is the most prevalent gas produced during a fire (reaching levels as high as 5 to 6 percent by volume), and its toxicity is attributed to its affinity for carboxyhemoglobin in the blood. Headaches can be experienced at concentrations of approximately 1,000 parts per million (PPM), while concentrations of 4,000 or more are fatal in less than an hour. Another common gas produced during a fire is carbon dioxide. Carbon dioxide is low in toxicity and is not normally considered a significant toxin in smoke. However, carbon dioxide does increase the speed and depth of breathing, thereby increasing carboxyhemoglobin in the blood from carbon monoxide.

Combustion of materials containing nitrogen bonds, such as wool and silk, leads to the release of hydrogen cyanide (HCN). The amount of HCN released is dependent on the temperature, with higher levels being generated at higher temperatures.

The toxicity of HCN is attributed to its ability to hinder cells from utilizing oxygen, a condition known as histotoxic hypoxia. Levels of HCN at 135 ppm are lethal within thirty minutes. It's important to note that during combustion, oxygen is consumed, which means that oxygen-deficient environments should be considered in terms of smoke toxicity. The typical concentration of oxygen in the air is 20.9%, and levels below 17% can cause diminished muscular control. In addition to the toxic effects of smoke, its impact on visibility should also be taken into account. Smoke obstructs the passage of light, potentially obstructing exits and impeding escape from a fire. The development of smoke in sufficient quantities to obscure exits occurs rapidly and is often the initial hazard in a fire. Moreover, eye irritation, primarily determined by the concentration of irritants in the smoke, can affect the vision of individuals attempting to escape.

Acetaldehyde	Irritates mucus membranes and eyes (colorless liquid)
Acrolein	Irritant, choking odor, extremely fatal (colorless-yellow liquid)
Asbestos	Causes asbestosis & lung cancer (fiber-like)
Benzene	Dizziness, excitation, headache, difficulty breathing, nausea, & vomiting (colorless liquid)
Bernzaldehyde	Irritant, bitter almond odor (colorless-yellow liquid)
Carbon Monoxide	Headache, dizziness, weakness, confusion, nausea, unconsciousness & death (colorless gas)
Formaldehyde	Irritant, pungent odor (colorless gas)
Glutaraldehyde	Severe irritation to eyes & skin (light-yellow liquid)

Hydrogen Chloride	Corrosive, sharp pungent odor (colorless gas)
Isovaleraldehyde	Respiratory distress, nausea, vomiting & headaches; suffocating odor (colorless liquid)
Nitrogen Dioxide	Highly toxic & corrosive (reddish-brown gas)
Particulates	Deposit in respiratory tract – irritant
Polycyclic Aromatic Hydrocarbons	Group of chemicals – carcinogen; pleasant odor (colorless, white or pale yellow)
Sulfur Dioxide	Toxic & corrosive; suffocating odor (colorless gas)

Carbon monoxide (CO) is produced when organic materials undergo incomplete combustion. It is a highly prevalent byproduct of combustion in structure fires. Exposure to carbon monoxide is often cited as the leading cause of death in civilian fire fatalities, as well as among firefighters who have depleted their air supply in self-contained breathing apparatus (SCBA). Carbon monoxide functions as a chemical asphyxiant by binding with hemoglobin in the blood, which hampers the transport of oxygen to the body's tissues.

Hydrogen cyanide (HCN) is another compound that is often present in smoke, although typically at lower concentrations compared to carbon monoxide (CO). It is produced during the combustion of materials containing nitrogen, such as certain types of furniture and bedding made from polyurethane. Hydrogen cyanide, like carbon monoxide, acts as a chemical asphyxiant, but it operates through a different mechanism. HCN inhibits the body's cellular utilization of oxygen, leading to a deprivation of oxygen at the cellular level. The significant presence of hydrogen cyanide in the combustion of polyurethane makes it an important consideration in fire safety and the potential hazards associated with smoke inhalation.

Carbon dioxide (CO2) is a byproduct of the complete combustion of organic materials. Unlike carbon monoxide and hydrogen cyanide, carbon dioxide is not toxic in the same manner. Instead, it acts as a simple asphyxiant by displacing oxygen in the air. High concentrations of carbon dioxide can lead to oxygen deprivation in enclosed spaces. However, in open areas, carbon dioxide quickly dissipates and does not pose a significant risk.

Additionally, carbon dioxide has a respiratory stimulant effect, meaning it can increase the rate of breathing. This response occurs as a natural physiological reaction to elevated carbon dioxide levels in the body. It is important to note that while carbon dioxide itself may not be highly toxic, its accumulation in confined spaces can still pose a hazard by reducing the available oxygen for breathing. Proper ventilation and monitoring are crucial to ensure a safe environment in situations where carbon dioxide may be present.

These are only a few examples of the common hazardous products of combustion that firefighters encounter. It is important to recognize that the toxic effects of smoke inhalation are not solely attributed to one specific gas, but rather the combined impact of all the present products.

Smoke contains irritants that can cause discomfort in breathing, inflammation of the eyes, respiratory tract, and skin. The specific irritants present in smoke can vary depending on the types of fuels involved in the fire.

Due to the potential lethality of the substances present in smoke from compartment fires, firefighters must use self-contained breathing apparatus (SCBA) to protect their respiratory system when operating in smoky environments. With their personal protective clothing and SCBA, firefighters perceive smoke as a lesser threat compared to heat and visible flames.

Flame is the visible, luminous body of burning gas. When a burning gas is mixed with an adequate amount of oxygen, the flame becomes hotter and less luminous. The reduced luminosity is a result of more complete combustion of carbon. Therefore, flame is considered one of the products of combustion. However, it should be noted that certain types of combustion, such as smoldering fires or glowing charcoal, do not produce a visible flame.

UNIQUE COMBUSTION PHENOMENA

During a fire, several unique combustion phenomena can occur, including explosions, deflagrations, detonations, flashovers, and back-drafts. Each of these phenomena has distinct characteristics and implications in fire safety.

An explosion refers to the rapid release of high-pressure gas into the surrounding environment. Unlike a typical fire, an explosion involves the sudden and intense release of energy. One example of an explosion during a fire is a boiling-liquid expanding-vapor explosion (BLEVE). Imagine a scenario where a fire reaches a flammable-liquid storage tank. The heat from the fire causes the liquid inside the tank to boil and generate vapor, leading to increased pressure. Emergency vents are designed to relieve this pressure. However, if the vents are unable to release the pressure quickly enough, the tank may fail, resulting in the release of the gas.

In industrial settings, most explosions are associated with combustion explosions, accounting for approximately 44% of incidents. These combustion explosions typically involve fuels and can be attributed to factors such as improper lighting procedures or inadequate safeguards on fuel appliances, such as low-gas shutoffs. Additionally, other sources of explosions in industrial settings include flammable-liquid vapors, combustible dusts, trapped steam, gas leakage, ruptured pressure vessels, nuclear or atomic explosions, and thermal explosions caused by unstable materials decomposing.

A **deflagration** refers to the burning or combustion of a gas or aerosol that is characterized by a combustion wave. In a deflagration, the combustion wave propagates through the mixture of fuel and oxygen, consuming the fuel until it is depleted. Unlike detonations, deflagrations do not produce a shock wave because the rate of travel of the combustion wave is less than the speed of sound.

Deflagrations are commonly associated with explosions that occur in industrial settings. They often involve the rapid combustion of flammable gases or aerosols, leading to the release of energy. The combustion process in a deflagration is relatively slower compared to detonations, where the combustion wave travels faster than the speed of sound, producing a shock wave.

It's important to understand and manage the risks associated with deflagrations in industrial environments. Proper handling, storage, and control of flammable gases or aerosols, along with implementing safety measures such as explosion-proof equipment, ventilation systems, and adherence to safety protocols, are essential for preventing and mitigating the potential hazards of deflagrations.

A **detonation** is a specific type of combustion phenomenon characterized by the rapid release of energy in the form of a shock wave. In a detonation, the combustion process occurs at an extremely high rate, with the shock wave propagating through the gas or aerosol faster than the speed of sound.

The shock wave generated by a detonation carries a significant amount of energy, resulting in a sudden increase in pressure and temperature. This high-pressure shock wave can cause damage to surrounding structures and materials. The intense heat and pressure created by the shock wave can also serve as a heat source, igniting other combustible materials in the vicinity, further contributing to the spread of fire.

Detonations are highly destructive and can occur in various scenarios, including industrial accidents, explosive devices, or certain chemical reactions. It's important to recognize the potential risks associated with detonations and take appropriate safety measures to prevent their occurrence or minimize their impact. This may involve proper storage and handling of explosive materials, implementing safety protocols, and using protective equipment in hazardous environments.

The following strategies are commonly employed to minimize the potential damage and hazards associated with explosive events.

1. Containment: Containment involves designing and constructing containers or vessels that are capable of withstanding the maximum pressure generated during an explosion. This can include using materials and engineering techniques that are resistant to pressure and fragmentation, ensuring that the structure can safely contain the explosion within its boundaries.

2. Quenching: Quenching refers to the process of removing heat or applying chemical inhibitors to halt the reaction that leads to an explosion. By reducing the temperature or introducing substances that inhibit the reaction, the progression of the explosion can be effectively stopped or slowed down.

3. Dumping: Dumping involves diverting or releasing the explosive materials or reaction to a controlled area that can handle the energy and potential hazards. This can be achieved by redirecting the flow of the explosive substances or releasing them in a manner that mitigates the impact and prevents further escalation.

4. Venting: Venting is the intentional release of energy and gases resulting from an explosion in a controlled manner. By providing a designated path for the pressure and gases to escape, the risk of

uncontrolled fragmentation or structural damage can be reduced. Venting systems are designed to direct the force of the explosion away from vulnerable areas.

5. Isolation: Isolation focuses on separating the process or area where an explosion may occur from surrounding areas that could be affected. This can be achieved through physical separation, such as distance or barriers, or through the use of blast-resistant structures that are designed to withstand and redirect the force of an explosion.

Implementing these methods for controlling explosions requires careful planning, risk assessment, and adherence to safety standards and regulations. It is essential to consult with experts and follow established guidelines to ensure the effectiveness of these measures in preventing or minimizing the impact of explosive events.

A **flashover** is indeed a significant and dangerous phenomenon that can occur during a fire in an enclosed space. It is characterized by the sudden ignition of the majority of combustible materials within the area, leading to a rapid and widespread fire. The key factor that triggers a flashover is the build-up of heat within the enclosed space.

During a fire, heat is released and accumulates in the surroundings. As the temperature rises, it reaches a point known as the ignition temperature, which is the minimum temperature at which a material will ignite and sustain combustion. In an enclosed space, the heat can become trapped and build up rapidly, causing the ambient temperature to rise.

When the ambient temperature reaches the ignition temperature of the majority of combustible materials present, a flashover can occur. At this point, the combustible materials within the space, including furniture, curtains, walls, and other contents, undergo spontaneous combustion almost simultaneously. This results in a sudden and intense fire that engulfs the entire area, often accompanied by a rapid release of energy and the development of thick smoke.

Flashovers pose a significant threat to both occupants and firefighters because of the sudden and intense fire conditions they create. It is crucial for firefighters to be aware of the signs and potential indicators of an imminent flashover, such as rapidly increasing temperatures, darkening or discoloration of the smoke, rollover flames, and the presence of pyrolysis gases.

Proper firefighting techniques, such as ventilation, cooling, and effective fire suppression strategies, are employed to prevent or control flashovers. Ventilation can help remove hot gases and reduce the build-up of heat, while cooling techniques aim to lower the temperature of the environment. Additionally, rapid and effective extinguishment of the fire is crucial to prevent further escalation and mitigate the risks associated with flashovers.

Firefighters undergo extensive training to recognize the signs of flashovers and implement appropriate strategies to safely manage these dangerous situations.

A **backdraft** is a dangerous combustion phenomenon that occurs in an enclosed area with limited oxygen supply. It occurs when a fire has depleted the available oxygen in a confined space, causing incomplete combustion and the production of large amounts of smoke and flammable gases, including carbon monoxide. When a sudden influx of fresh air is introduced, such as by opening a door or breaking a window,

the mixture of fuel-rich gases and oxygen can ignite rapidly and explosively, resulting in a backdraft. The explosion-like effect is caused by the rapid combustion of accumulated flammable gases, including carbon monoxide, in the presence of oxygen. Backdrafts pose a significant risk to firefighters and can cause severe injuries or fatalities. Proper ventilation techniques and an understanding of fire behavior are crucial in preventing and managing backdraft situations.

FIRE TRIANGLE

Fire triangle, which consists of oxygen, fuel, and heat, has long been used as a basic model to understand fire and its requirements. In this model, the presence of all three components is necessary for a fire to initiate and sustain.

Oxygen is necessary to support the combustion process by providing the oxidizer. Fuel refers to any combustible material that can undergo a chemical reaction with oxygen to release heat and produce flames. Heat is the energy required to raise the temperature of the fuel to its ignition point and maintain the self-sustaining chemical reaction.

The fire triangle provides a reasonable explanation of non-flaming or smoldering combustion.

However, it is important to note that the fire triangle is a simplified representation and does not encompass all aspects of fire behavior. In some cases, additional factors and conditions can influence fire behavior and its extinguishment.

FIRE TETRAHEDRON

The fire tetrahedron is an extension of the fire triangle that includes a fourth component: a self-sustained chemical chain reaction. The fire tetrahedron provides a more comprehensive model for understanding flaming combustion and the factors involved in its initiation and sustenance.

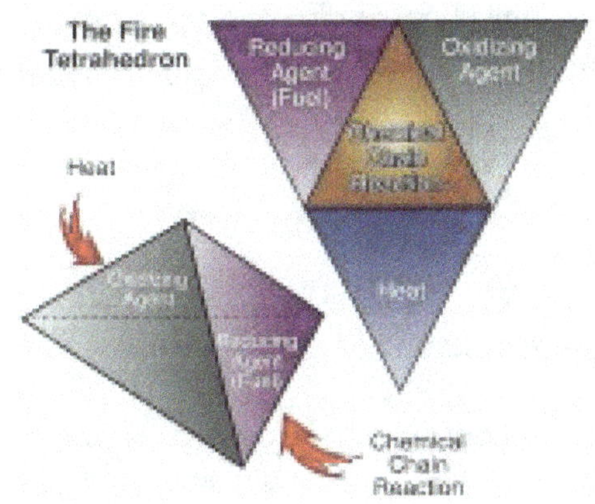

In addition to the presence of oxygen, fuel, and heat, the self-sustained chemical chain reaction is crucial for the continuation of flaming combustion. This chemical chain reaction involves the interaction between fuel molecules, oxygen, and heat, producing combustion products and releasing additional heat, which sustains the fire.

If any of the components of the fire tetrahedron are removed, the flaming combustion process can be interrupted or extinguished. For example, removing the fuel source, reducing or eliminating the oxygen supply, or cooling the heat below the ignition temperature can lead to fire extinguishment.

However, it's important to note that even if the flaming combustion is extinguished, the fuel may continue to smolder if the conditions are favorable for smoldering combustion. Smoldering combustion involves slow, low-temperature oxidation of fuel without the presence of visible flames. It can persist in materials such as charcoal, embers, or certain organic substances, and may reignite if conditions change.

Understanding both the fire triangle and the fire tetrahedron provides a more comprehensive understanding of fire behavior and helps inform firefighting strategies and fire safety practices.

HEAT AND TEMPERATURE

Heat and temperature are often used interchangeably, but they have distinct meanings in the context of fire behavior and thermodynamics.

Heat refers to the transfer of thermal energy from one object or substance to another due to a temperature difference. It is the energy in transit, flowing from a hotter object to a colder object until thermal equilibrium is reached. Heat transfer can occur through various mechanisms such as conduction, convection, and radiation.

On the other hand, temperature is a measure of the average kinetic energy of the particles in a substance. It represents the intensity of heat present in an object or substance. Temperature is measured using a scale such as Celsius or Fahrenheit and is typically represented by a numerical value.

In simple terms, heat is the energy being transferred, while temperature is a measure of the intensity of that energy.

In the context of fire behavior, heat is a critical component. The heat generated during combustion raises the temperature of the surrounding materials, causing them to reach their ignition temperature and sustain the fire. Understanding the transfer of heat and how it affects the temperature of fuels and the environment is crucial for assessing fire growth, spread, and control.

So, while heat and temperature are related concepts, they have distinct meanings and play different roles in understanding fire behavior and thermodynamics.

ENERGY

Energy is the capacity to do work, and work involves the application of a force over a distance or the transformation of a substance.

In the context of heat, energy is transferred from one object to another, and this transfer can result in an increase in temperature. The measurement of energy is typically done indirectly by measuring the work done or the effects it produces.

In the International System of Units (SI), the standard unit for measuring energy is the joule (J). One joule is defined as the amount of energy transferred when a force of one newton is applied over a distance of one meter. This unit is widely used to measure various forms of energy, including heat energy.

So, when heat is involved, the energy transferred can be quantified in joules, and this measurement helps us understand the amount of work that the heat energy can do, such as increasing the temperature of a substance.

UNIT OF MEASURE

The British thermal unit (Btu) is commonly used as a unit of measure for heat. The Btu is defined as the amount of heat required to raise the temperature of one pound of water by one degree Fahrenheit. It is still frequently used in certain industries, including the fire service.

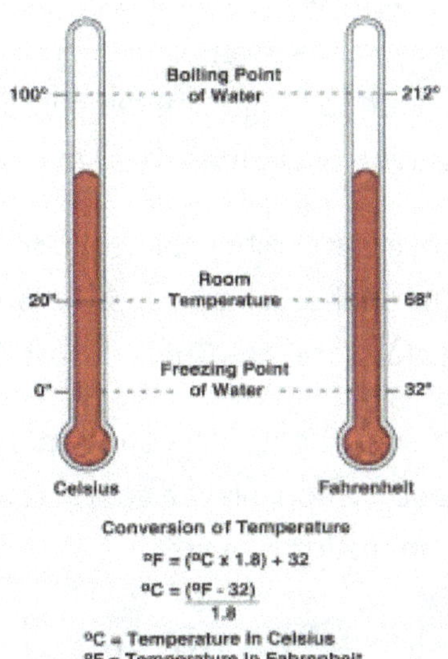

Regarding temperature scales, you are also correct that there are different scales used to measure temperature. The Celsius scale is part of the metric system and is widely used in scientific and engineering contexts around the world. The freezing point of water is defined as 0 degrees Celsius (°C), while the boiling point of water is defined as 100°C at standard atmospheric pressure.

In contrast, the Fahrenheit scale is used in the customary system, primarily in the United States and a few other countries. On the Fahrenheit scale, the freezing point of water is defined as 32 degrees Fahrenheit (°F), and the boiling point of water is defined as 212°F at standard atmospheric pressure.

Comparing the two scales, we can see that the Celsius scale has a more logical and consistent interval, as the difference between the freezing and boiling points of water is 100 units. The Fahrenheit scale, on the other hand, has a larger interval between the two points, with a difference of 180 units. However, it's worth noting that both scales are still in use, and conversion between them can be done using specific formulas or conversion tables.

In summary, the British thermal unit (Btu) is commonly used as a unit of measure for heat in the customary system, while the Celsius and Fahrenheit scales are used to measure temperature, with the Celsius scale being part of the metric system and the Fahrenheit scale used in the customary system.

ENERGY AND HEAT ROLE IN FIRE BEHAVIOR

Energy plays a crucial role in fire behavior, and the conversion of energy into heat is a significant factor in the fire tetrahedron. When a fuel is exposed to heat, its temperature increases, leading to various chemical processes.

In solid fuels, such as wood, heat can cause pyrolysis, which is the chemical decomposition of the fuel due to the action of heat. Pyrolysis breaks down complex organic compounds in the fuel into simpler volatile compounds, such as gases, vapors, and tars. These volatile components are then available for combustion.

In the case of liquid fuels, such as gasoline or oil, heat causes vaporization. As the liquid fuel is heated, it evaporates, forming ignitable vapors that can mix with air to create a flammable mixture. These vapors, when ignited, contribute to the sustained combustion process.

The introduction of an external source of ignition, such as a spark, flame, or hot surface, can provide the necessary activation energy to initiate the combustion reaction. However, in some cases, the fuel can be heated to its ignition temperature without the need for an external ignition source. This is known as self-ignition or spontaneous ignition.

Once the combustion reaction is initiated, it becomes self-sustaining. The heat generated from the burning fuel further releases more vapors and gases, which continue to ignite, creating a chain reaction that sustains the fire. This self-sustaining nature of the combustion process is an essential characteristic of fires.

Overall, the conversion of energy into heat, along with the subsequent processes of pyrolysis and vaporization, plays a critical role in fuel preparation and ignition, ultimately leading to the sustained combustion of a fire.

FORMS OF IGNITION

There are two forms of ignition: piloted ignition and autoignition, both of which can occur under fire conditions.

Piloted ignition, as you mentioned, happens when a mixture of fuel and oxygen encounters an external ignition source, such as a flame, spark, or hot surface, with sufficient heat energy to initiate the combustion reaction. The external ignition source provides the necessary activation energy to start the reaction, and once ignited, the fire sustains itself by the continuous supply of fuel, oxygen, and heat.

Autoignition, on the other hand, occurs without any external flame or spark to ignite the fuel gases or vapors. Instead, the fuel surface is heated to a temperature at which the combustion reaction spontaneously occurs. This heating can be the result of high ambient temperatures, radiant heat from nearby flames, or exothermic reactions within the fuel itself. The temperature at which autoignition takes place is known as the autoignition temperature (AIT) of the substance. The AIT is always higher than the piloted ignition temperature.

While both forms of ignition can occur in fire situations, piloted ignition is more common. It is often facilitated by readily available ignition sources present in the environment, such as open flames, sparks, or hot surfaces. Autoignition typically requires specific conditions, including high temperatures, fuel characteristics, and confinement, for the ignition temperature to be reached without the aid of an external ignition source.

Understanding the differences between piloted ignition and autoignition is important for fire safety and prevention measures, as it helps in identifying the potential ignition sources and assessing the fire hazards associated with different materials and environments.

HEAT ENERGY SOURCES

1. Chemical Heat Energy: Chemical reactions, particularly oxidation reactions, are the most common source of heat in combustion. When a combustible material comes into contact with oxygen, oxidation occurs, resulting in the production of heat. This chemical heat energy is responsible for sustaining and propagating fires.

2. Mechanical Heat Energy: Mechanical heat energy is produced through friction or compression. Friction between two surfaces in relative motion generates heat, which can lead to ignition or spark formation. Heat of compression is generated when a gas is compressed, and it can be utilized in certain applications, such as diesel engines igniting fuel vapor without a spark plug.

3. Self-heating, or spontaneous heating, occurs when a material increases in temperature without the addition of external heat. Heat is produced slowly by oxidation, typically through chemical reactions, and is usually lost to the surroundings as fast as it is generated. However, certain conditions can initiate or accelerate the self-heating process. For self-heating to progress to spontaneous ignition, the following factors are required:

   - Insulation Properties: The material surrounding the fuel must have insulation properties that restrict the dissipation of heat. This means that the heat generated cannot escape as quickly as it is produced.

   - Heat Production Rate: The rate at which heat is produced must be sufficient to raise the temperature of the material to its ignition temperature. As more heat is generated and held by the insulating materials, the rate of the oxidation reaction increases, leading to higher heat production.

   - Air Supply (Ventilation): Adequate air supply or ventilation is necessary to support combustion. Sufficient oxygen must be available to sustain the oxidation reactions that generate heat.

An example illustrating the potential for spontaneous ignition is oil-soaked rags rolled into a ball and placed in a corner. If the heat generated by the natural oxidation of the oil and cloth is not allowed to dissipate, either through air movement or other heat transfer mechanisms, the temperature of the cloth can gradually increase. When the heat generated exceeds the heat lost, the material may reach its ignition temperature and ignite spontaneously.

The rate at which most chemical reactions occur doubles with approximately every 18°F (10°C) increase in temperature. Therefore, as more heat is generated and absorbed by the fuel, the reaction rate accelerates, leading to faster heat production. Once the heat generated surpasses the heat being lost, the material can reach its ignition temperature and ignite spontaneously.

Understanding self-heating and the conditions for spontaneous ignition is crucial for fire safety and prevention. Proper storage and handling of materials prone to self-heating, along with adequate ventilation and heat dissipation measures, can help mitigate the risk of spontaneous ignition and potential fires.

4. Electrical heat energy: Electrical heating can lead to temperatures high enough to ignite combustible materials in the vicinity of the heated area. There are several ways in which electrical heating occurs:

- Resistance Heating: When an electric current flows through a conductor, heat is produced due to the resistance offered by the material. Some electrical appliances, such as incandescent lamps, ranges, ovens, or portable heaters, are specifically designed to utilize resistance heating. These devices employ materials with high resistance to generate heat when the current passes through them.
- Overcurrent or Overload: When the current flowing through a conductor exceeds its intended design limits, it can overheat and pose a risk of ignition. Overcurrent or overload conditions lead to unintended resistance heating, causing excessive heat buildup in the electrical system.
- Arcing: Arcing refers to a high-temperature luminous electric discharge that occurs across a gap or through a medium, such as charred insulation. Arcs can be generated in various situations, such as when a conductor is separated (e.g., in an electric motor or switch) or due to high voltage, static electricity, or lightning. Arcing can result in intense heat and pose a fire hazard if combustible materials are present in the vicinity.
- Sparking: Sparking refers to the formation of electrically charged particles that emit a luminous glow and spatter away from the point of arcing. Sparks can be generated during electrical disturbances or faulty connections, and they can ignite nearby combustible materials.

It is important to recognize the potential hazards associated with electrical heating and take appropriate precautions to minimize the risk of ignition. This includes proper design, installation, and maintenance of electrical systems, as well as avoiding overloading circuits and ensuring good electrical connections. Fire safety measures, such as using electrical devices within their intended operating conditions and promptly addressing any electrical issues or malfunctions, are essential for preventing electrical-related fires.

TRANSMISSION OF HEAT

Heat transfer plays a fundamental role in the study of fire behavior, and understanding how heat is transmitted from one point or object to another is crucial for firefighters to assess and respond to fires effectively.

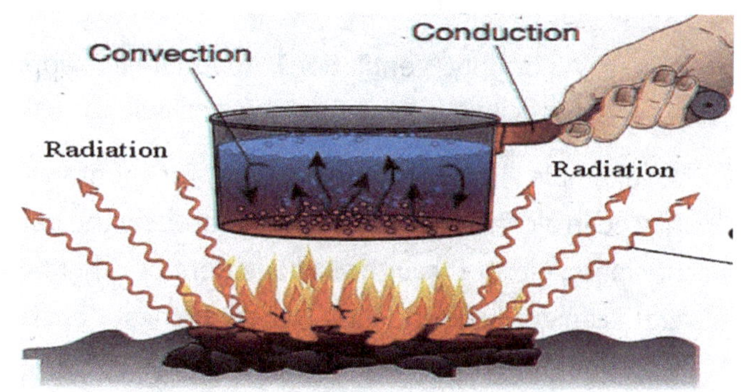

In order for heat to be transferred, there must be a temperature difference between two bodies or objects. Heat naturally flows from a region of higher temperature to a region of lower temperature, seeking thermal equilibrium. This temperature differential drives the transfer of heat energy.

In the context of fire behavior, heat is generated at the source, which is typically the initial fuel package or burning object. As this fuel burns, it releases heat energy. This heat can then be transferred to other nearby fuels, causing them to heat up and potentially ignite. The transfer of heat to surrounding fuels contributes to the growth and spread of the fire.

Firefighters rely on their understanding of heat transfer to estimate the size and potential spread of a fire before engaging in firefighting operations. By assessing the temperature differentials and the path of heat transfer, they can make informed decisions about the appropriate tactics and resources needed to control and extinguish the fire. Additionally, evaluating the effectiveness of their firefighting efforts involves monitoring changes in temperature and heat transfer patterns.

There are three mechanisms for transfer of heat which are conduction, convection and radiation. They are discussed below.

Conduction

Conduction is indeed the transfer of heat within a body or between bodies in direct contact. It occurs primarily in solids, where heat is transferred through molecular collisions and increased molecular motion.

For example, the metal pipe being heated by a fire on one side can conduct heat to the other side of the wall. The heat energy is transferred from the hot side of the pipe to the cooler side through the metal's molecular structure. If there are wooden framing components or combustible materials in contact with the other side of the wall, the conducted heat can raise their temperature, potentially leading to ignition and the spread of fire.

Conduction is influenced by factors such as the thermal conductivity of the material, which determines how readily it conducts heat. Metals, with their closely packed and highly conductive atomic structures, are efficient conductors of heat. Insulators, on the other hand, have low thermal conductivity and impede the transfer of heat.

The thermal conductivity of a material plays a significant role in heat transfer through conduction. The thermal conductivity refers to a material's ability to conduct heat and is usually expressed in units of watts per meter-kelvin (W/m·K). A higher thermal conductivity indicates that the material is more effective at conducting heat.

Here's an example table showcasing the thermal conductivity of various common materials at a standard ambient temperature of 68°F or 20°C:

Material Thermal Conductivity (W/m·K)

- Copper 401
- Aluminum 237
- Steel (Stainless) 15-45
- Iron 80
- Glass 1-1.4
- Concrete 0.8-1.7
- Wood (Oak) 0.17
- Plastic (Polyethylene) 0.35-0.5

As you can see, materials like copper and aluminum have high thermal conductivities, making them excellent conductors of heat. Steel and iron also exhibit relatively high thermal conductivities compared to materials like glass, concrete, wood, and plastic.

Considering the above figures mentioned, a steel-frame building will conduct heat more readily than a wood-frame building due to the difference in thermal conductivity between steel and wood. This means that heat will transfer more easily through the steel structure, potentially affecting the spread of fire or the distribution of heat within the building.

Insulating materials are designed to impede the transfer of heat, primarily by slowing down conduction between two bodies. Good insulators are typically materials that have low thermal conductivity, meaning they do not conduct heat efficiently.

Insulating materials work by disrupting the direct transfer of heat energy from one point to another. They achieve this by utilizing their physical composition to inhibit heat flow. One effective approach is to use materials composed of fine particles or fibers that create void spaces filled with a gas, such as air. Gases, in general, have low thermal conductivity because the molecules within them are relatively far apart, limiting the ability to transfer heat through molecular collisions.

By incorporating materials with low thermal conductivity and utilizing trapped air or other insulating gases, the transfer of heat by conduction can be significantly slowed down. This is a key principle in building construction, where insulating materials are employed to reduce heat transfer through walls, roofs, and other structural components.

It's important to note that insulation also plays a role in mitigating heat transfer by other mechanisms, such as convection and radiation. However, the disruption of conduction is one of the primary mechanisms by which insulators retard the transfer of heat.

Understanding the thermal conductivity of different materials helps in various aspects of fire safety and design, such as selecting appropriate building materials, implementing insulation strategies, and assessing the potential for heat transfer and structural integrity in fire situations.

Understanding the process of conduction is vital in fire safety and prevention. By identifying potential pathways for heat transfer through conduction, such as pipes, walls, or other solid objects, appropriate measures can be taken to minimize the risk of ignition or the spread of fire to nearby combustible materials. This knowledge helps firefighters assess the potential for heat transfer and take appropriate actions to control and extinguish fires effectively.

Conviction

Convection is another important mechanism of heat transfer in the context of fire. It involves the transfer of heat energy through the movement of a fluid, such as a liquid or gas, to a solid surface. In the case of a fire, convection primarily occurs through the movement of hot smoke and fire gases.

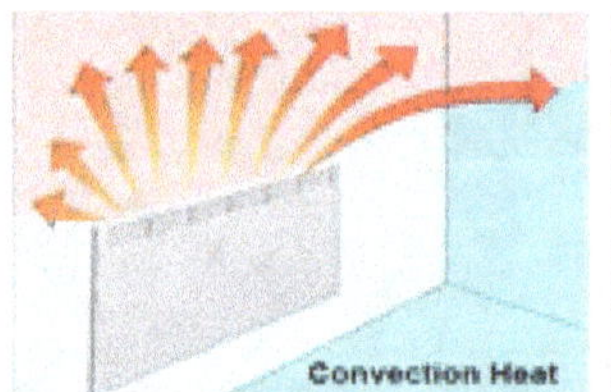

As a fire grows and fuels burn, the surrounding air is heated. The hot air and combustion products become buoyant due to their reduced density compared to the surrounding cooler air. This causes them to rise and create upward air currents. These rising currents carry heat energy along with them.

Convection plays a significant role in spreading heat within a fire environment. The hot smoke and fire gases transfer heat to the surrounding surfaces, including structural materials, building contents, and the surrounding air. This heat transfer occurs as the hot gases come into contact with these cooler surfaces, transferring their heat energy through convection.

Convection can contribute to fire growth and the spread of fire to other areas by carrying heat to new fuel sources. It also influences the behavior of fire, such as the formation of fire plumes, smoke movement, and the development of thermal layers within a structure.

Understanding the principles of convection and its impact on heat transfer is essential for firefighters and fire safety professionals in assessing fire behavior, predicting fire spread, and implementing effective firefighting strategies.

Radiation

Radiation is indeed an important mechanism of heat transfer in the context of fire. It involves the transmission of energy as electromagnetic waves, such as light waves, radio waves, or X-rays, without the need for a medium to carry it.

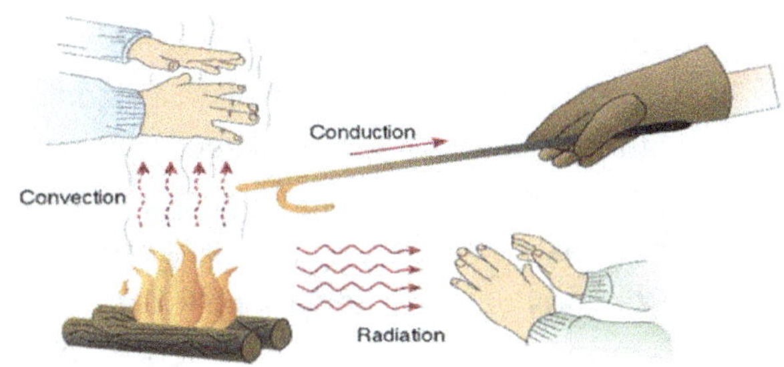

In the case of fire, thermal radiation is the primary form of radiation involved. It occurs as a result of the temperature of the fire and all matter above absolute zero. Any object or surface with a temperature above absolute zero radiates heat energy in the form of electromagnetic waves.

Radiant heat transfer becomes particularly significant as a fire grows in size. The heat energy in the form of thermal radiation can travel in straight lines and can reach objects located at a distance from the fire. This radiation can directly heat up and ignite combustible materials without the need for direct contact or convection.

The impact of radiant heat transfer on fire behavior and spread is significant. It can lead to the ignition of objects and surfaces that are not in direct contact with the flames or heated gases. As radiant heat is absorbed by combustible materials, their temperature increases, potentially reaching their ignition point and causing them to ignite.

Various factors play a crucial role in influencing radiant heat transfer. Understanding these factors is essential for assessing fire behavior and implementing appropriate fire safety measures. Here are the key factors that affect radiant heat transfer:

1. Nature of Surfaces: The properties of the surfaces involved, such as their color and texture, impact the absorption and emission of radiant heat. Dark-colored materials tend to absorb and emit heat more effectively than light-colored materials. Smooth or highly polished surfaces have higher reflectivity, meaning they reflect more radiant heat compared to rough surfaces.

2. Distance between Surfaces: The distance between the heat source and the surfaces being heated affects the intensity of radiant heat. As the distance increases, the intensity of radiant heat decreases. The inverse square law governs the relationship between radiant heat and distance, stating that the intensity of radiant heat is inversely proportional to the square of the distance.

3. Temperature Difference: The temperature difference between the heat source and the objects being heated significantly influences radiant heat transfer. The radiant energy emitted by a heat source increases with the fourth power of the temperature difference. This means that even small changes in temperature can have a substantial impact on the radiant heat transfer. Doubling the temperature results in a sixteen-fold increase in radiant heat energy.

Radiant heat transfer is unique because it can occur through a vacuum or air spaces, unlike conduction and convection which require a medium for heat transfer. Here are some additional points to consider:

1. Speed of Transmission: Radiant heat travels at the speed of light, allowing for rapid energy transfer over large distances. This is evident in the heat we receive from the sun, which travels through the vacuum of space to reach the Earth's surface.
2. Exposure Fires: Radiation plays a significant role in exposure fires, where the heat from a fire ignites objects or fuel packages that are not directly in contact with the original fire source. As a fire grows and releases more energy, it radiates heat in all directions, potentially igniting combustible materials at a considerable distance.
3. Ignition Potential: Radiant heat can ignite materials by raising their temperature to the point of ignition. When radiant heat energy is absorbed by an object, it increases the kinetic energy of its molecules, eventually reaching the ignition temperature if sufficient heat is received.
4. Reflective Surfaces: Certain materials have reflective properties that can disrupt the transmission of radiant heat. Reflective surfaces bounce back a significant portion of the radiant energy, reducing the amount of heat absorbed by the material. This property can be advantageous in fire safety measures by providing a barrier against radiant heat exposure.

Passive agents

In addition to fuel, heat, and oxygen, there are other materials that can influence fire ignition and development. Passive agents are substances that absorb heat but do not actively participate in the combustion process. Fuel moisture, which refers to the water content in combustible materials, is an example of a passive agent that hinders the absorption of heat and delays ignition and combustion. For instance, a well-hydrated shrub will take longer to catch fire compared to a dehydrated one.

Relative humidity and fuel moisture are significant factors in the development of wildland fires, but the impact of passive agents is also noteworthy in structural fires. For instance, the presence of passive agents can affect the rate of fire spread in different types of buildings. In a newly constructed wood-frame building where the wood is still relatively green, a fire may not propagate as rapidly as in an older building where the framing members have dried out over time. Understanding the role of passive agents is crucial for comprehending fire development and assessing the effectiveness of fire control tactics aimed at mitigating the risk of rapid fire progression.

FUEL (REDUCING AGENT)

Fuel is the material or substance that undergoes oxidation or combustion in the combustion process. It plays a vital role in the radiating agent of a combustion reaction. Fuels can be categorized as inorganic or organic. Inorganic fuels, such as hydrogen or magnesium, do not contain carbon, while organic fuels do contain carbon. The majority of common fuels are organic and consist of carbon along with other elements. These fuels can be further classified into hydrocarbon-based fuels (e.g., gasoline, fuel oil, and propane) and cellulose-based materials (e.g., wood and paper).

The physical state and distribution or orientation of the fuel are two important factors that influence the combustion process. Fuels can exist in the gas, solid, or liquid states. Flaming combustion requires fuels to be in the gaseous state. The conversion of solids and liquids into gases requires the input of heat energy.

Gaseous Fuel

Gaseous fuels, such as methane (natural gas), hydrogen, acetylene, and others, can be particularly hazardous because they are already in a state that is readily ignitable. Gases possess mass but lack a definite shape or volume. When contained within a vessel, a gas will disperse and fill the available space. Upon release, gases will either rise or sink based on their density compared to that of air. Lighter-than-air gases, like methane, have a tendency to rise, while heavier-than-air gases, like propane (liquefied petroleum gas), have a tendency to sink.

Vapor density is a measure of a gas's density relative to air. Air is assigned a vapor density of 1. Gases with a vapor density below 1 will ascend, while those with a vapor density exceeding 1 will descend. These densities assume that the gas and air are at the same temperature, typically specified as 68°F (20°C). When heated, gases expand and become less dense, whereas cooling causes them to contract and become denser. The following table provides characteristics of some common flammable gases.

Liquid Fuel

Liquids possess both mass and volume but lack a definite shape, conforming to the shape of their container with a flat surface. When released, liquids will flow in the direction of gravity and can accumulate in lower areas. Similar to gases being compared to air, the density of liquids is compared to that of water. Specific gravity denotes the ratio of the mass of a given volume of liquid to the mass (weight) of an equal volume of water at the same temperature. Water is assigned a specific gravity of 1. Liquids with a specific gravity less than 1, such as gasoline and most flammable liquids (though not all), are lighter than water and will float on its surface. Conversely, liquids with a specific gravity greater than 1, like epichlorohydrin (used in plastic production), are heavier than water. Therefore, water can be employed to exclude oxygen from a burning liquid.

The process of burning liquids requires their transformation into vapor or a gaseous state through vaporization. At sea level, the atmosphere applies a pressure of approximately 14.7 psi (102.9 kPa).

To undergo vaporization, liquids must surpass the pressure exerted by the atmosphere. Vapor pressure refers to the pressure generated or exerted by the vapors emitted from a liquid. As a liquid is heated, both vapor pressure and the rate of vaporization increase. For instance, a puddle of water eventually evaporates. However, when the same amount of water is heated on a stove, it vaporizes much more quickly due to the greater amount of energy being applied. The rate of vaporization is determined by the vapor pressure of the substance and the amount of heat energy supplied to it. The volatility or ease with which a liquid releases vapor affects its susceptibility to ignition.

The flash point of a liquid is the temperature at which it releases enough vapors to ignite when exposed to an ignition source, but the combustion is not sustained. On the other hand, the fire point is the temperature at which sufficient vapors are generated to sustain the combustion reaction once ignited. The flash point is often used as an indicator of the flammability risk associated with liquid fuels. Liquid fuels that can vaporize enough to ignite at temperatures below 100°F (38°C) pose a significant flammability hazard.

The surface area of a liquid exposed to the atmosphere plays a role in the vaporization process. In open containers, the surface area available for vaporization is often limited. However, if a liquid is released and allowed to flow onto the ground, it will spread out and pool in low areas. This increased surface area of the liquid exposed to the atmosphere leads to a corresponding increase in the production of fuel vapors. The larger the surface area, the more vapors can be generated, which can pose a greater flammability risk.

The density of a liquid compared to water and its solubility are important characteristics that firefighters consider when dealing with liquid fuels. Hydrocarbon fuels like gasoline, diesel, and fuel oil are lighter than water and do not mix with it. On the other hand, polar solvents such as alcohols (e.g., methanol and ethanol) readily mix with water.

The solubility of a liquid describes how well it can mix with water. It can be expressed qualitatively (slightly or completely) or quantitatively as a percentage. When dealing with water-soluble liquids, using water as an extinguishing agent can pose challenges. Applying water to such liquids can increase the volume of the liquid, potentially spreading the fire. Additionally, some water-based extinguishing agents like certain types of firefighting foam can mix with water-soluble liquids, rendering them ineffective. Therefore, specialized extinguishing agents may be required in these situations.

Solid fuels

Solids have a definite size and shape, and their behavior when exposed to heat can vary. Some solids, like wax, thermoplastics, and metals, can undergo a change of state and melt when heated, while others, like wood and thermosetting plastics, do not melt.

Solid fuels release fuel gases and vapors through a process called pyrolysis, which is the chemical decomposition of a substance due to heat. When solid fuels are heated, they undergo pyrolysis, resulting in the release of combustible vapors and gases. If there

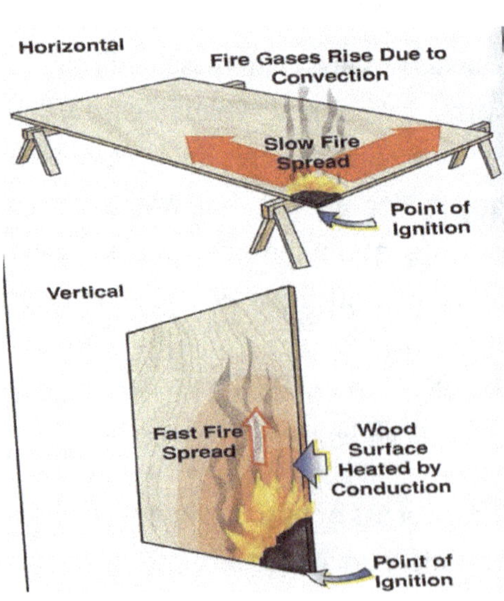

is enough fuel and heat, these gases can ignite when in the presence of sufficient oxygen or another oxidizer.

In a fire that occurs in a room or enclosed space, the primary fuels are often solid materials such as wood, paper, or plastic. Pyrolysis is a critical process in generating the flammable vapors and gases needed for combustion. When wood is heated, it initially releases water vapor as the moisture content evaporates. As the heating continues, the wood undergoes pyrolysis, breaking down into its volatile components and carbon.

Pyrolysis of solid fuels typically begins at temperatures below 400°F (204°C). This process involves the chemical decomposition of the fuel due to heat, resulting in the release of combustible vapors and gases. However, it's important to note that the ignition temperature of the vapors being given off during pyrolysis is higher, ranging approximately from 1,000°F to 1,300°F (538°C to 704°C).

When it comes to synthetic fuels such as plastics, the process of pyrolysis is similar to that of wood. However, unlike wood, plastics generally do not contain moisture that needs to be evaporated by heat before pyrolysis can occur. Therefore, plastics can undergo pyrolysis more readily once they are exposed to sufficient heat.

The surface-to-mass ratio of solid fuels plays a significant role in their ignitability. Solid fuels, unlike liquids or gases, have a definite shape and size, and this characteristic affects their ease or difficulty of ignition.

The surface-to-mass ratio refers to the amount of surface area relative to the mass of the fuel. A higher surface-to-mass ratio means there is a larger surface area exposed to the surrounding environment compared to the mass of the fuel. This increased surface area allows for more efficient heat transfer and interaction with oxygen, which in turn enhances the fuel's ignitability.

To illustrate this concept, let's consider the example of a large tree being transformed into different forms of wood products. A felled tree has a low surface-to-mass ratio since its surface area is relatively small compared to its mass. However, when the tree is sawn into planks, the resulting surface area increases, thereby increasing the surface-to-mass ratio. Further processing, such as milling or sanding, generates shavings or sawdust with an even higher surface-to-mass ratio. These finely divided particles have a significantly increased ignitability due to their large surface area, which allows for faster generation of combustible pyrolysis products when exposed to heat.

The proximity and orientation of solid fuel in relation to the heat source have a significant impact on the way it burns. Let's consider the example of a sheet of 1/8-inch plywood paneling to illustrate this point.

When the plywood paneling is laid horizontally (flat) and ignited from one corner, the fire consumes the fuel at a relatively slow rate. In this orientation, the heat from the fire is primarily transferred to the fuel through conduction and radiation. The heat has to travel across the surface of the paneling to reach the unburned areas, which slows down the fire development.

However, if the same type of paneling is positioned vertically (standing on edge) and ignited from the bottom, the fire burns much more rapidly. In this case, the proximity of the solid fuel to the heat source is much closer, allowing for more efficient heat transfer. The heat is directly applied to the surface of the paneling, increasing the rate of pyrolysis and combustion. The vertical orientation allows the heat to rise and preheat the unburned portion above, creating a self-sustaining fire.

The vertical position of the paneling enhances the contact between the heat source and the solid fuel, resulting in faster fire development. This effect can be observed in many scenarios where the orientation and proximity of solid fuels to the heat source play a critical role in the speed and intensity of the fire.

HEAT OF COMBUSTION AND HEAT RELEASE RATE

The chemical composition of a fuel has a significant impact on its heat of combustion and heat release rate (HRR). Let's delve into these concepts further:

Heat of combustion refers to the total amount of energy released when a specific quantity of fuel undergoes complete oxidation or combustion. It is a measure of the potential heat energy contained within the fuel. The heat of combustion is typically expressed in units of energy per unit mass, such as kilojoules per gram (kJ/g). Different fuels have different heat of combustion values, depending on their chemical makeup. For instance, many plastics, flammable liquids, and flammable gases have higher heat of combustion values compared to wood. This is an important consideration for firefighters, given the prevalence of synthetic materials in building construction and contents.

Heat release rate (HRR) represents the amount of energy released per unit of time as a fuel burns. It is a measure of how quickly heat is generated during the combustion process. HRR is commonly expressed in units of power, such as kilowatts (kW). The heat release rate is influenced by various factors, including the type, quantity, and arrangement of the fuel. The characteristics of the fire's enclosure, if it is burning within a compartment, can also impact the heat release rate. In most fires, the heat release rate changes over time, increasing as more fuel becomes involved and then declining as the available fuel is consumed.

Understanding the heat of combustion and heat release rate is crucial for firefighters because it helps them assess the potential intensity and progression of a fire. These factors influence the heat output, flame spread, and overall behavior of the fire. By considering the chemical content of different fuels and their corresponding heat release rates, firefighters can make informed decisions and develop effective strategies to control and extinguish fires.

Representative Peak Heat Release Rate (HRR) During Unconfined Burning

FUEL MATERIAL	PEAK HRR IN KILOWATTS	COMMON LOCATIONS FOR MATERIAL
SMALL WASTEBASKET	4-18	Homes, business, shops
COTTON MATTRESS	140-350	Homes, furniture stores, motels
COTTON EASY CHAIR	290-370	Homes, furniture stores, office building
SMALL POOL OF GASOLINE	400	Traffic crash, fuel stations
DRY CHRISTMAS TREE	500-650	Homes, trash facilities, dumpster, recycling sites
POLYURETHANE MATTRESS	810-2630	Homes, furniture stores, motels, dormitories and jails
POLYURETHANE EASY CHAIR	1350-1990	Homes, furniture stores, motels
POLYURETHANE SODA	3120	Homes, furniture stores, motels, dormitories, office building

OXYGEN (OXIDIZING AGENT)

Oxygen is the primary oxidizing agent in most fires. It plays a crucial role in the combustion process by reacting with the fuel to produce heat, light, and various combustion byproducts. In our atmosphere, the air we breathe typically contains about 20.9 percent oxygen.

In addition to oxygen, there are other materials known as oxidizers that can support combustion in a similar manner. Oxidizers are substances that facilitate the oxidation of a fuel by providing oxygen or other oxygen-rich compounds. While oxidizers themselves are not combustible, they enhance the combustion process by supplying the necessary oxygen for the reaction to occur.

Examples of oxidizers include chemicals like hydrogen peroxide, chlorine, potassium permanganate, and ammonium nitrate. These substances can react with fuels and sustain the combustion process by releasing oxygen or oxygen-containing compounds that readily participate in the chemical reaction.

Common Oxidizers

SUBSTANCE	COMMON USE
CALCIUM HYPOCHLORITE (GRANULAR SOLID)	Chlorination of water in swimming pools
CHLORINE (GAS)	Water purification
AMMONIUM NITRATE (GRANULAR SOLID)	Fertilizer
HYDROGEN PEROXIDE	Industrial bleaching (pulp and paper chemical & manufacturing)
METHYL ETHYL KETONE PEROXIDE	Catalyst in plastics manufacturing

It's important to note that in the context of fire safety, it's crucial to handle oxidizers with caution as they can significantly increase the intensity and rate of combustion when combined with a fuel source.

The concentration of oxygen in the atmosphere plays a crucial role in fire behavior and poses risks to both fire safety and human survival. At normal ambient temperatures (around 70°F or 21°C), materials can ignite and burn with oxygen concentrations as low as 14 percent. In such oxygen-limited environments, the combustion process may shift to surface or smoldering mode, where flames are less visible but still present.

However, it's important to note that at high ambient temperatures, flaming combustion can continue even at considerably lower oxygen concentrations. Surface combustion, characterized by slower and less intense burning, can persist at extremely low oxygen concentrations, even in relatively cool environments.

Safety regulations define an atmosphere with less than 19.5% oxygen as oxygen-deficient and hazardous for individuals without proper respiratory protection, such as self-contained breathing apparatus (SCBA) that provides a supply of fresh air. On the other hand, when the oxygen concentration exceeds 23.5%, the atmosphere is classified as oxygen-enriched, which increases the risk of fire.

In oxygen-enriched atmospheres, materials exhibit different burning characteristics compared to normal oxygen levels. Substances that burn in normal oxygen levels will burn more intensely and may even ignite spontaneously in oxygen-enriched atmospheres. For example, petroleum-based materials can autoignite in such environments. Additionally, materials that are non-combustible in normal oxygen levels may readily burn in oxygen-enriched atmospheres. Nomex® fire-resistant fabric, commonly used in the construction of protective clothing for firefighters, is one such material. While it does not burn in normal oxygen levels, it ignites and burns vigorously when exposed to an oxygen-enriched atmosphere of approximately 31 percent oxygen.

Understanding the influence of oxygen concentration is crucial for fire safety measures, as it affects fire behavior, combustion characteristics of materials, and the choice of appropriate protective equipment in different environments.

The following table describes flammable ranges for some materials. It's important to note that these values are approximate and can vary depending on factors such as temperature, pressure, and specific chemical composition. It's always recommended to consult reliable references such as chemical handbooks, safety data sheets (SDS), and relevant standards and regulations for accurate and up-to-date information on flammable limits of specific materials.

Additionally variations in temperature and pressure can affect the flammable range, with increases in temperature or pressure generally broadening the range and decreases in temperature or pressure narrowing it. These should be taken into account when assessing fire hazards & implementing measures.

1. Methane (natural gas):
    - Lower Flammable Limit (LFL): 5%
    - Upper Flammable Limit (UFL): 15%
2. Propane:
    - LFL: 2.1%
    - UFL: 9.5%
3. Gasoline:
    - LFL: 1.4%
    - UFL: 7.6%
4. Ethanol (ethyl alcohol):
    - LFL: 3.3%
    - UFL: 19%
5. Acetone:
    - LFL: 2.6%
    - UFL: 12.8%
6. Hydrogen:
    - LFL: 4%
    - UFL: 75%

SELF-SUSTAIN CHEMICAL REACTION

This process is complex and involves the formation of free radicals, which are highly reactive species that play a crucial role in the chain reaction.

When a fuel such as methane reacts with oxygen, the initial reaction produces free radicals such as methyl radicals ($CH_3\cdot$) and hydroxyl radicals ($OH\cdot$). These radicals then react with other fuel molecules or with oxygen, leading to the formation of intermediate combustion products and more free radicals. This chain reaction continues as long as there is a sufficient supply of fuel, oxygen, and heat.

The combustion process of complex fuels involves a wide range of radicals and intermediate products, which can vary depending on the specific fuel composition. Some of these intermediate products, like carbon monoxide and formaldehyde, can be flammable and toxic, posing additional hazards in fires.

To extinguish a fire, it is necessary to disrupt the self-sustaining chemical reaction. This can be achieved by removing one or more of the essential components required for combustion, such as fuel, oxygen, or heat. Extinguishing agents can act by cooling the fuel and reducing the temperature below the ignition point, displacing or diluting the oxygen concentration, or interfering with the chemical reaction itself.

Chemical flame inhibition, as you mentioned, involves the use of extinguishing agents that interfere with the chain reaction and form stable products that are not readily reactive. Halon-replacement extinguishing agents, for example, can disrupt the chain reaction by interacting with the free radicals and inhibiting further combustion.

It's important to note that the use of certain extinguishing agents, such as Halon, has been phased out due to their adverse environmental effects. There are now alternative agents and suppression systems available that are designed to be effective while also being more environmentally friendly.

Flaming combustion involves a self-sustaining chemical chain reaction that rapidly releases heat, light, and combustion products. This rapid heat generation leads to the ignition and sustained burning of a fuel. In contrast, slower oxidation reactions, such as rusting or yellowing, occur at a much slower rate and do not generate sufficient heat to reach the ignition point or sustain a fire.

Surface combustion refers to oxidation reactions occurring at the surface of a fuel material without the presence of visible flames. Glowing charcoal briquettes are a classic example of surface combustion. In this case, the charcoal reacts with oxygen in the air, generating heat and producing glowing embers. Surface combustion differs from flaming combustion in that it lacks the presence of open flames and the associated self-sustaining chemical chain reaction.

When dealing with surface combustion, extinguishment methods need to focus on one or more components of the fire triangle: heat, fuel, and oxygen. Methods such as cooling the fuel source, removing the fuel or oxygen supply, or physically separating the burning material from its surroundings can be effective in extinguishing surface fires. Chemical flame inhibition agents, which interfere with the chemical chain reaction in flaming combustion, are not effective in extinguishing surface combustion since there are no visible flames or sustained chain reactions to disrupt.

CLASSIFICATION OF FIRE

Understanding the classification of fires is crucial because each class has unique extinguishment requirements. This overview will briefly discuss the five fire classes and their relationship to the fire tetrahedron. For more comprehensive information, refer to the manual's dedicated chapters on fire control and extinguishment.

Class A fires

Class A fires encompass common combustible materials like wood, cloth, paper, rubber, grass, and various plastics. When dealing with Class A fires, the primary method of extinguishment involves cooling the fuel to lower its temperature, thereby impeding or halting the release of pyrolysis products. Cooling is effective in suppressing the combustion process and preventing re-ignition.

Class B fires

Class B fires pertain to flammable and combustible liquids and gases like gasoline, oil, lacquer, paint, mineral spirits, and alcohol. In the case of Class B fires involving gases, the fire can be extinguished by isolating and shutting off the gas supply. For fires involving Class B liquids, the application of foam or dry chemical agents, in a suitable manner, is effective in extinguishing the fire. These agents work by smothering the fire, interrupting the oxygen supply, and suppressing the release of flammable vapors.

Class C fires

Class C fires are unique because they involve energized electrical equipment. Typical sources of Class C fires include household appliances, computers, transformers, electric motors, and overhead transmission lines. It's important to note that electricity itself does not burn, so the actual fuel in a Class C fire is usually the insulation on wiring (which is considered Class A material) or lubricants (which are considered Class B materials).

When dealing with a Class C fire, it is recommended to de-energize the involved electrical equipment whenever possible before attempting to extinguish the fire. This helps to eliminate the ignition source and reduce the risk of electrocution. If de-energizing is not immediately possible, it is crucial to use an extinguishing agent that does not conduct electricity. This is to ensure the safety of the individuals involved in extinguishing the fire and to prevent further electrical hazards.

Class D fires

Class D fires are specific to combustible metals, including aluminum, magnesium, potassium, sodium, titanium, and zirconium. These metals can be highly hazardous, especially in their powdered form. When airborne metal dust reaches the right concentrations and encounters an appropriate ignition source, it can lead to powerful explosions.

It's important to note that the extremely high temperatures generated by burning metals can cause water to react and other common extinguishing agents to be ineffective. Therefore, standard approaches to fire suppression may not work for Class D fires. No single extinguishing agent is universally effective in controlling fires involving all types of combustible metals.

Dealing with Class D fires requires specialized extinguishing agents specifically designed for combating fires involving combustible metals. These agents are often in the form of dry powders, such as sodium chloride, graphite, or powdered copper, which can smother the fire and interrupt the chemical reactions. Proper training and knowledge of the specific metal involved are essential when addressing Class D fires to ensure effective and safe suppression measures.

Class K fires

Class K fires are specific to fires involving oils and greases typically found in commercial kitchens and food preparation facilities where deep fryers are used. Extinguishing these fires requires the use of agents specifically formulated for the materials involved.

The extinguishing agents designed for Class K fires work through a process called saponification. Saponification is a chemical reaction that converts fats and oils into a soapy substance, which effectively extinguishes the fire. These agents are typically based on potassium acetate or potassium citrate, and they are specifically formulated to combat the unique challenges posed by fires fueled by cooking oils and greases.

When a Class K fire occurs, it is crucial to use the appropriate fire suppression system and extinguishing agent designed for these types of fires. These systems are typically equipped with specialized nozzles that discharge the agent in a manner that optimizes its effectiveness. In addition to using the correct extinguishing agent, it is important to follow proper safety procedures, such as shutting off the heat source and ensuring the area is properly ventilated.

Given the unique nature of Class K fires and the potential hazards involved, it is recommended that individuals working in commercial kitchens or food preparation facilities receive proper training on fire safety, including the use of fire suppression systems and extinguishing agents designed for Class K fires.

FIRE DEVELOPMENT IN A COMPARTMENT

Fire development in a compartment, which refers to an enclosed room or space within a building, follows a distinct pattern influenced by the confinement of the fire and the interactions between heat, fuel, and the surrounding environment.

When a fire occurs in an unconfined area, much of the heat generated during the combustion process is dissipated into the atmosphere through radiation and convection. However, in a confined compartment, the walls, floors, and objects within the space absorb a portion of the radiant heat produced by the fire. The remaining radiant heat that is not absorbed is reflected back into the compartment, further increasing the temperature of the fuel and promoting a higher rate of combustion.

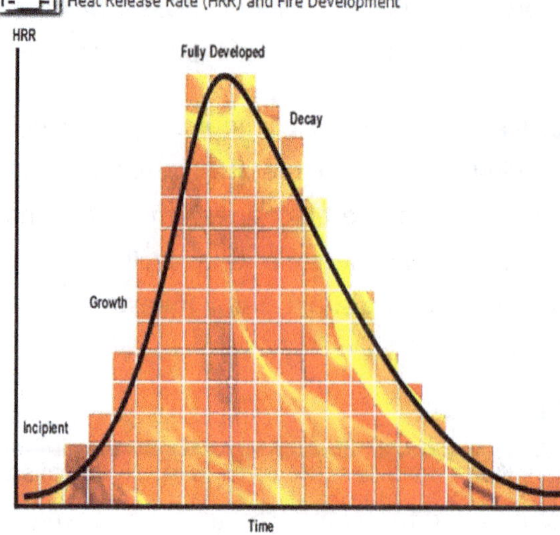

As the fire burns, the hot smoke and air generated by the fire become buoyant and rise. Upon contact with cooler materials such as the ceiling and walls of the compartment, heat is transferred through conduction, raising the temperature of these materials. This heat transfer process gradually elevates the temperature of all combustible materials present in the compartment.

As nearby fuel sources are exposed to the increasing temperatures, they undergo pyrolysis, a process in which they are decomposed by heat into volatile gases. These gases, along with the surrounding oxygen, create an environment where flaming combustion can be sustained and the fire can spread. The rate of pyrolysis and flaming combustion increases as the temperature rises, leading to a self-sustaining fire that extends further within the compartment.

It's important to note that the specific progression of fire development in a compartment can vary based on various factors such as the size and configuration of the space, the types of materials present, and the availability of oxygen. Nonetheless, understanding the impact of confinement on fire behavior helps firefighters assess the situation, develop effective strategies for suppression, and prioritize safety measures to control and extinguish the fire.

When there is an ample supply of oxygen, the development and behavior of a fire are primarily influenced by the properties and arrangement of the fuel involved. In this situation, the fire is considered to be fuel controlled. The characteristics of the fuel, such as its combustibility, surface area, and arrangement, play a significant role in determining the fire's growth and spread within the compartment.

As the fire progresses and consumes available fuel, it may reach a stage where the primary factor limiting its development is the availability of fresh air or ventilation. When this occurs, the fire is referred to as ventilation controlled. The restricted air supply hampers the fire's ability to sustain and intensify its combustion process.

In a ventilation-controlled fire, the limited air supply can have important implications for firefighting operations. Altering the ventilation conditions, such as opening or closing doors and windows, can significantly impact the fire's behavior. Increasing the air supply to a ventilation-controlled fire can result in rapid fire growth and increased hazards for firefighters, while reducing the air supply can help control and suppress the fire.

Fire development in a compartment can be characterized by several stages, although it is important to note that the boundaries between these stages are not always precisely delineated, especially in real-world scenarios outside of controlled laboratory conditions. Nonetheless, these stages serve as a useful framework for firefighters to comprehend the progression of a fire within a confined space. The stages typically identified are incipient, growth, fully developed, and decay.

Incipient stage

The incipient stage of a fire begins with the ignition, which occurs when the three elements of the fire triangle (fuel, heat, and oxygen) combine, leading to combustion. Ignition can be initiated by a spark, flame, or self-heating of a material, such as spontaneous ignition when a substance reaches its autoignition temperature. In the incipient stage, the fire is typically small and contained to the initially ignited material, and it may self-extinguish.

Once combustion starts, the development of an incipient fire is primarily influenced by the characteristics and arrangement of the fuel involved, making it a fuel-controlled fire. Sufficient oxygen from the surrounding air supports the continuous growth of the fire. In this initial phase, radiant heat from the fire begins to heat adjacent fuel, causing it to undergo pyrolysis (decomposition by heat). A plume of hot gases and flames rises from the fire and mixes with the cooler air in the room through convection.

As the plume reaches the ceiling, the hot gases spread horizontally across the ceiling, a phenomenon referred to as a ceiling jet in scientific terms (commonly known as mushrooming among firefighters). The hot gases in contact with the surfaces of the compartment and its contents transfer heat through conduction, raising the temperature of other materials, including additional fuel. This intricate process of heat transfer contributes to an overall increase in the room's temperature during the incipient stage of the fire.

During the incipient stage of fire development, the impact of the fire on the compartment environment is still relatively minimal. The temperature inside the compartment is only slightly higher than the ambient temperature, and the concentration of combustion products is low. In this stage, occupants can safely evacuate from the compartment, and the fire can be effectively extinguished using portable fire extinguishers or small hose lines.

However, it is crucial to understand that the transition from the incipient stage to the growth stage can happen rapidly, sometimes within a matter of seconds. The speed of this transition depends on factors such as the type of fuel involved and its configuration within the compartment. It emphasizes the importance of prompt action and swift intervention during the early stages of a fire to prevent its escalation and control it effectively before it progresses to a more advanced stage.

As a fire progresses from the incipient stage to the growth stage, it starts to have a greater impact on the environment within the compartment. At the same time, the configuration of the compartment and the amount of ventilation present also influence the behavior of the fire. In a compartment fire, the interaction between the fire and the ceiling and walls plays a significant role.

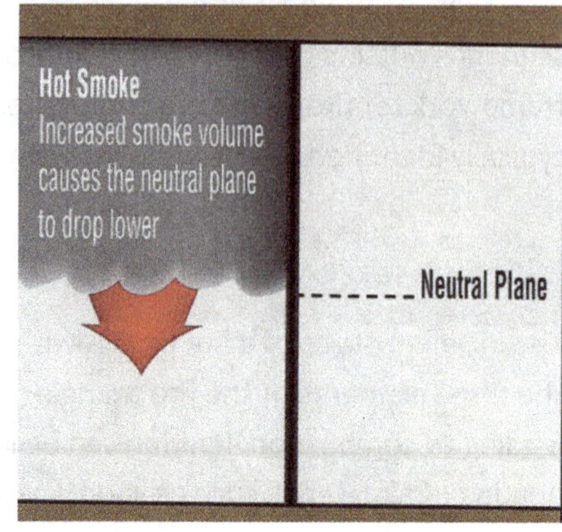

.One of the first effects is the entrainment of air into the plume of hot gases rising from the fire. In unconfined fires, where air can be drawn from all sides, the entrainment of air helps to cool the plume, resulting in reduced flame length and vertical extension of the fire.

However, in a compartment fire, the location of the fuel package in relation to the compartment walls determines the amount of air that can be entrained and the level of cooling that occurs. If the fuel package is near the walls, it can only entrain air from three sides, while fuel packages located in corners can only entrain air from two sides. As a result, the combustion zone expands vertically, leading to higher plume temperatures. This, in turn, further stretches the combustion zone and increases the plume temperatures even more. The temperatures in the developing hot-gas layer above the fire are significantly affected by this phenomenon, influencing the speed of fire development.

Furthermore, as the surfaces of the compartment walls become hot, the burning fuel receives more reflected radiant heat. This additional heat contributes to the acceleration of fire development, intensifying the fire's growth and progression.

Overall, the configuration of the compartment, including the location of fuel packages and the presence of walls, plays a crucial role in the entrainment of air, cooling of the plume, and the subsequent development and spread of the fire within the compartment.

THERMAL LAYERING

As a fire develops within a compartment, the heated products of combustion, along with the entrained air, become buoyant and rise to the ceiling in the form of a plume. When these hot gases reach the ceiling, they spread horizontally, creating a "ceiling jet" that moves through the compartment. This spreading continues until the gases reach the walls of the compartment. As the combustion process persists, the depth of the gas layer increases.

The thermal layering phenomenon occurs as a result of the difference in density between the hot smoke and the cooler air below. This causes the gases to separate into two distinct layers based on their temperature. The upper layer consists of the hottest gases, while the lower layer contains the cooler gases. This stratification of gases according to temperature is also referred to as heat stratification or thermal balance.

In addition to the heat transfer through radiation and convection, as mentioned earlier, the radiation emitted by the hot gas layer further contributes to heating the interior surfaces of the compartment and its contents. This radiation can cause an increase in temperature in the compartment, influencing the spread and intensity of the fire.

The thermal layering and the resulting temperature distribution within the compartment play a significant role in fire behavior and firefighting tactics. Firefighters need to be aware of this layering effect to effectively assess the conditions inside the compartment and make informed decisions regarding fire suppression and ventilation strategies.

As the hot gas layer within the compartment grows in volume and temperature, its pressure also increases. This higher pressure causes the hot gas layer to exert force downward and outward, seeking any available openings such as doors or windows to escape.

In contrast, the cool gas layer has lower pressure, leading to the inward movement of air from outside the compartment. When the hot and cool gas layers meet at an opening, such as a doorway or window, the pressure is neutral at that interface. This interface is commonly known as the neutral plane.

It's important to note that the term "neutral plane" specifically refers to the interface between the hot smoke and the cooler air when hot gases are exiting the compartment and cooler air is entering. The neutral pressure only exists in this scenario.

In firefighting operations, it is generally preferable to maintain or raise the level of the hot gas layer above the floor. By doing so, a more tenable environment can be created for firefighters and trapped occupants. Achieving this goal requires effective implementation of fire control and ventilation tactics, such as proper use of firefighting techniques and strategic opening of ventilation points to control the flow of hot gases and facilitate their removal from the compartment.

ISOLATED FLAMES

During the growth stage of a fire, it is possible to observe pockets of flames moving through the hot gas layer located above the neutral plane. This phenomenon is often referred to as "ghosting." Ghosting occurs when portions of the hot gas layer within the flammable range encounter sufficient temperature for ignition. As these hot gases circulate towards the outer edges of the plume, they find an adequate oxygen supply to sustain combustion and ignite. It is important to note that ghosting occurs before more substantial involvement of flammable combustion products within the hot gas layer.

Ghosting is classified as a fire gas ignition event and serves as an indicator of potential flashover conditions. Flashover is a critical

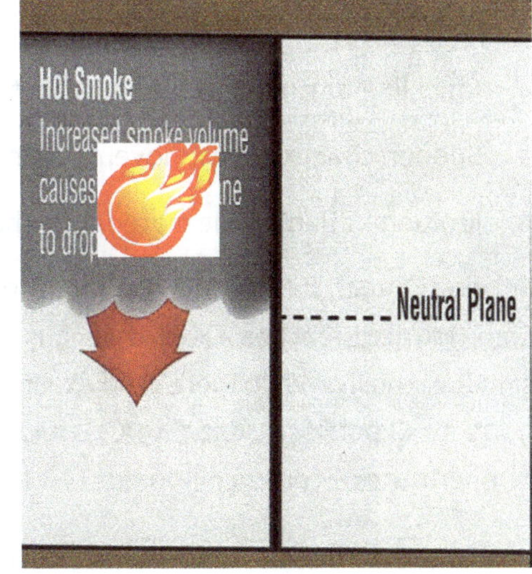

event in which the contents of a compartment reach their ignition temperature almost simultaneously, resulting in rapid and widespread fire growth. When ghosting is observed, it signifies the likelihood of developing flashover conditions. Firefighters must take immediate action to prevent flashover by implementing effective firefighting strategies, such as rapid cooling techniques and ventilation control, to manage the fire's progression and reduce the risk of a catastrophic event.

FLASHOVER

Flashover is indeed a rapid transition that occurs between the growth and fully developed stages of a fire. It is characterized by a significant change in the conditions within the compartment, leading to the involvement of the entire space. Although flashover is not an ignition event itself, it represents a critical moment in the fire's progression.

During flashover, the fire's growth becomes more intense and widespread, resulting in a sudden release of burning gases from the compartment's openings, such as doors or windows, at a high velocity. This release is accompanied by a rapid increase in temperature and radiant heat emission.

Flashover can occur almost instantaneously, catching firefighters off guard. The movement of flames and hot gases during flashover can be faster than the escape speed of firefighters. The radiant heat produced during a flashover is extremely intense and can be fatal within a matter of seconds, even for firefighters wearing full personal protective equipment (PPE) and self-contained breathing apparatus (SCBA).

There are several indicators that can help predict the occurrence of flashover, including:

1. Rapidly increasing heat and temperature within the compartment.

2. Thick, turbulent smoke filling the room.

3. Flames rolling across the ceiling (rollover).

4. Crackling or rumbling sounds from the fire.

5. Sudden changes in air movement and drafts.

6. Ignition of flammable materials in the vicinity without direct flame contact.

For firefighters, flashover is commonly defined as the moment when the temperature within a compartment reaches a level that causes all the combustible contents in the space to ignite simultaneously. While there is no exact temperature associated with flashover, a range of approximately 900°F to 1,200°F (483°C to 649°C) is widely recognized. This temperature range aligns with the autoignition temperature of carbon monoxide (CO), which is one of the most common gases produced during pyrolysis.

Leading up to flashover, several critical changes occur within the burning compartment. The temperatures rise rapidly, additional fuel becomes involved in the fire, and the fuel present in the compartment releases combustible gases due to pyrolysis. When flashover happens, the combustible materials in the compartment and the gases produced by pyrolysis ignite almost simultaneously. This results in the entire room becoming fully involved in the fire.

Understanding the indicators and conditions preceding flashover is crucial for firefighters to recognize the potential for this extremely dangerous event. By closely monitoring temperature, fuel involvement, and the presence of combustible gases, firefighters can take proactive measures to prevent or mitigate the impact of flashover.

It's essential to consider multiple indicators and evaluate the overall fire conditions rather than relying on a single indicator. Understanding the big picture is crucial for firefighters to effectively assess the situation and make informed decisions.

During flashover, the intense heat generated can lead to disorientation and cause severe thermal burns. Firefighters must remain constantly aware of the evolving fire conditions and employ appropriate strategies to manage the risks associated with flashover. This includes implementing effective fire control techniques and ventilation tactics to control the fire environment.

Maintaining situational awareness, closely monitoring fire behavior, and staying in communication with fellow firefighters are vital for managing the risks posed by flashover. By continuously assessing the changing conditions and implementing appropriate control measures, firefighters can reduce the potential for flashover and ensure their own safety while working to extinguish the fire.

FOOD FOR THOUGHT!

Flashover does not occur in every compartment fire, and the likelihood of flashover depends on two interrelated factors: heat energy and ventilation.

The first factor, heat energy, refers to the amount of heat released by the fire and its ability to increase the temperature within the compartment. The heat energy produced by a fire must reach a certain threshold to create the conditions necessary for flashover. A small fire, such as the ignition of paper in a metal wastebasket, may not generate enough heat energy to lead to flashover in a large room with significant thermal mass, such as gypsum drywall. However, a fire involving highly flammable materials like polyurethane foam cushions on a couch can release a substantial amount of heat energy and have a higher potential for flashover.

The second factor, ventilation, plays a critical role in the progression to flashover. Adequate oxygen supply is necessary for a fire to reach flashover conditions. A sealed or poorly ventilated room restricts the availability of oxygen, limiting the fire's ability to rapidly escalate to flashover. Insufficient ventilation can result in the fire entering the growth stage but not reaching the peak heat release associated with a fully developed fire.

When a fire becomes ventilation controlled, the heat release rate is reduced due to limited oxygen availability. However, despite the reduced heat release, the temperature within the compartment can still continue to rise, although at a slower pace compared to when the fire was fuel controlled.

If ventilation is increased, either through the failure of window glazing or when firefighters make entry and introduce additional air, it can lead to a sudden increase in heat release. The influx of fresh air provides more oxygen for the fire, causing the heat release rate to rise rapidly in some cases. This can result in a dangerous escalation of the fire conditions and poses risks for firefighters and occupants in the vicinity.

A fire can quickly become ventilation-controlled, which means that the available oxygen becomes the limiting factor for the rate of burning. When the fire becomes ventilation-controlled, the temperature of the compartment may still rise, but the heat release rate will be reduced. However, if ventilation is increased, such as through a broken window or a door opened by firefighters, additional air can rapidly increase the heat release rate and the fire can intensify very quickly. Even with open doors and windows, a fire can become ventilation-controlled if there is insufficient air supply to support the fire's growth. The resulting smoke will be rich in unburned fuel, which can create a highly flammable and explosive atmosphere in the compartment.

Fully developed stage

The fully developed fire stage is characterized by the burning of all available combustible materials in the compartment. At this stage, the fire is ventilation controlled, meaning that the heat release is dependent on the availability of oxygen through the compartment openings. The fire is producing a significant amount of heat and generating large volumes of fire gases. If there is an increase in the available air supply, such as through additional ventilation or the opening of doors or windows, the heat release rate can further increase.

In the fully developed stage, the hot fire gases can flow from the compartment of origin into adjacent compartments or escape through openings in the building's exterior. As these hot gases enter spaces with more abundant air, they may ignite and cause fire gases ignition. This can lead to the rapid spread of the fire to other areas of the building. It is important for firefighters to be aware of these potential pathways for fire spread and take appropriate measures to control and extinguish the fire.

Decay stage

When the fuel in a compartment fire is consumed, the combustion reaction will slow and eventually stop. This can occur if the fire has reached its limit in terms of available fuel, or if firefighters have successfully extinguished the fire using water or another extinguishing agent.

On the other hand, if the oxygen concentration in the compartment falls to a point where flaming combustion can no longer be supported, the fire will also decay. This can occur in a closed compartment where the available oxygen has been consumed or in an open compartment where ventilation has been limited.

However, decay due to reduced oxygen concentration can follow a different path if the ventilation profile of the compartment changes. If, for example, a window is opened or a door is breached, fresh air can enter the compartment, providing oxygen to the remaining fuel and reigniting the fire. Therefore, it is important for firefighters to closely monitor the ventilation profile of a fire and adjust their tactics accordingly to prevent unexpected reignition.

BACKDRAFT

In a ventilation-controlled compartment fire, the incomplete combustion of fuels can generate a significant volume of flammable smoke and gases. This mixture of flammable products can accumulate within the compartment, often exceeding their upper flammable limits. While the heat release rate may be limited, the temperatures within the compartment can still remain high.

If there is a sudden increase in ventilation, such as by opening a door or window, it can introduce the necessary oxygen to the fuel-rich environment. This rapid influx of oxygen can lead to a deflagration, commonly known as a backdraft. A backdraft occurs when the accumulated flammable gases ignite almost instantly, resulting in a rapid and explosive combustion.

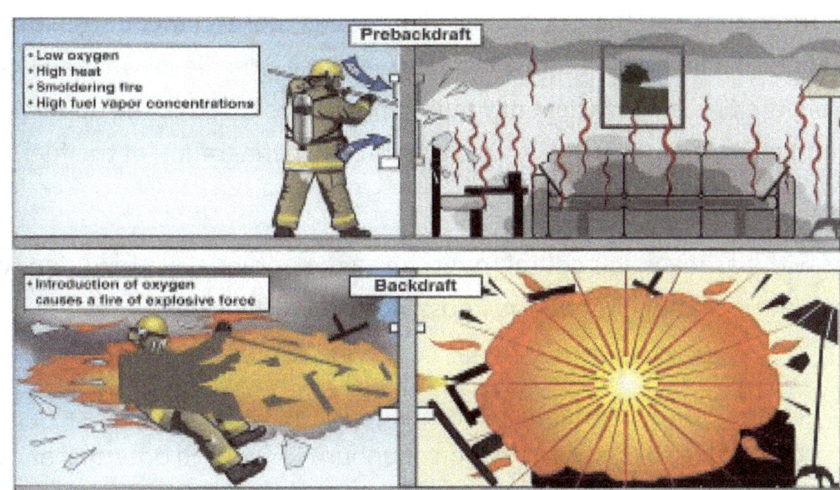

To clarify, the conditions for a backdraft typically involve a compartment filled with unburned fuel (smoke) that is already at or above its ignition temperature but lacks sufficient oxygen to sustain combustion. Opening a horizontal opening, such as a door, can provide the necessary oxygen, causing the trapped fuel and gases to ignite rapidly, leading to a backdraft event.

A backdraft can occur without the reaction of a horizontal opening. The key factor is the mixing of hot, fuel-rich smoke with air, which can lead to the ignition and rapid combustion of the trapped gases. Backdraft conditions can develop within a room, a void, or an entire building, wherever there is a buildup of hot combustion products and insufficient oxygen for combustion.

It is essential to consider the potential for backdraft before creating any openings into a compartment or space that contains extremely hot combustion products. The violent nature of a backdraft can be influenced by the degree of confinement of the fuel/air mixture. When the deflagration is more confined, such as in a smaller space, the release of energy can be more intense and result in a more violent backdraft event.

Firefighters must exercise caution and evaluate the conditions carefully to assess the potential for backdraft before introducing additional air or creating openings. Understanding the signs and indicators of backdraft, such as smoke puffing, pressurized smoke, or a sudden increase in fire activity, is crucial for maintaining firefighter safety and effectively managing firefighting operations.

Backdrafts pose a significant hazard to firefighters and can result in sudden and intense fire spread, as well as potential structural damage. Firefighters must be aware of the signs and indicators of potential backdraft conditions

Backdraft conditions can occur in compartments that are not completely filled with hot products of combustion. In large-volume and high-ceiling compartments, the fire may be burning above the hot gas layer, creating the potential for backdraft conditions in the upper levels of the compartment, even if conditions at the floor level are not severely affected.

In such scenarios, the hot gases and unburned fuel accumulating in the upper portion of the compartment can reach a flammable concentration, while the lower levels may still have a relatively moderate impact from the fire. If a sufficient oxygen supply is introduced to the upper level, such as through an opening or ventilation, it can result in a rapid ignition and deflagration of the fuel-rich mixture, leading to a backdraft event.

As with flashover, it is critical to recognize the potential warning signs of backdraft conditions. Common indicators of the potential for a possible backdraft include:

1. Smoke leaving the building in puffs: This refers to smoke being expelled from the building intermittently, rather than a continuous flow. It may indicate a restricted ventilation path, which can contribute to the accumulation of unburned fuel and potential backdraft conditions.

2. Little or no visible flame: Backdraft conditions are often characterized by a lack of visible flames, as the available oxygen may be insufficient to sustain open combustion. Instead, the fire may be smoldering and producing large amounts of flammable smoke.

3. Inwardly drawn smoke (sucking phenomenon): Backdraft conditions can cause smoke to be drawn inward into the building or compartment, rather than flowing outward. This is a result of pressure differentials created by the potential fuel-rich mixture.

4. Black smoke becoming dense gray-yellow: The color and density of smoke can change as backdraft conditions develop. Initially, the smoke may be black and sooty, but as the fuel-rich mixture forms, it can become denser and take on a gray or yellowish hue.

5. Pressurized smoke exiting small openings: Backdraft conditions can cause smoke to be expelled forcefully from small openings, such as gaps around doors or windows. This is due to the pressure buildup within the compartment.

6. Smoke-stained windows with heat-induced cracking of glass: The intense heat and pressure associated with backdraft conditions can lead to visible signs on windows, such as smoke staining or even cracking of the glass due to thermal stress.

It's important to note that these indicators are not definitive proof of an impending backdraft, but they serve as warning signs that firefighters should be aware of. Proper assessment, continuous monitoring, and adherence to firefighting tactics and procedures are crucial to ensure firefighter and occupant safety when faced with potential backdraft conditions.

Pulsing smoke movement is generally acknowledged as a common indicator of a potential backdraft, whereas the raising and lowering of the neutral plane is not typically considered as such. However, it is important to note that when the compartment or structure is not completely filled with smoke, alterations in pressure and smoke volume can cause fluctuations in the position of the neutral plane. Instead of the characteristic pulsing discharge of smoke from openings, changes in the neutral plane may be observed. These variations in the neutral plane can occur due to factors like ventilation, thermal conditions, and airflow patterns within the space. Firefighters should be mindful of these dynamics and consider a combination of indicators when assessing the potential for a backdraft. While pulsing smoke movement remains a widely recognized indicator, understanding the changes in pressure, volume, and movement of smoke can provide additional insights into the presence of backdraft conditions.

It is also important to highlight that the occurrence of a backdraft is not always immediate or imminent after making an opening into the involved compartment. The mixing of hot flammable products of combustion with air can be influenced by factors such as gravity currents, pressure differentials, and wind effects, which may take time to develop. In such situations, it is advisable for firefighters to delay entry until appropriate actions are taken to modify the conditions inside the building or compartment, such as gas cooling with hose streams or implementing vertical ventilation techniques.

The effects of a backdraft can indeed vary significantly based on several factors, including the volume of flammable products of combustion, degree of confinement, the speed of fuel-air mixture, and the location of ignition. These variables can impact the violence and severity of the backdraft event.

It is crucial for firefighters to maintain situational awareness, continuously assess conditions, and make informed decisions to mitigate the risks associated with backdraft situations.

FACTORS AFFECTING FIRE DEVELOPMENT

FUEL TYPE

The type of fuel plays a critical role in fire development. Combustible materials that have a high surface-to-mass ratio are more susceptible to ignition and tend to burn at a faster rate compared to materials with less surface area. This means that fuels with a larger exposed surface area, such as fine wood shavings or paper, can ignite more easily and support a more rapid combustion process.

Furthermore, the moisture content of ordinary combustibles like wood and paper greatly affects their burn ability. When these materials are wet or contain significant moisture, the heat energy that would otherwise contribute to the process of pyrolysis, where the fuel decomposes and releases flammable gases, is absorbed by the water present in the fuel. This absorption of heat hinders the ignition process and reduces the fuel's ability to sustain a rapid and intense fire.

Conversely, dry fuels with low moisture content are more prone to ignition and support faster combustion. Dry wood or paper, for instance, ignite more readily due to the absence of moisture that would otherwise absorb heat energy. These dry fuels can rapidly release combustible gases and contribute to the spread and intensity of a fire.

AVAILABILITY AND LOCATION OF ADDITIONAL FUEL

Building configuration plays a crucial role in determining the availability and location of additional fuels during a fire. Factors such as the layout of the structure, number of stories, presence of fire spread avenues, compartmentation, and barriers to fire spread all impact the potential for fire to access and involve additional fuels. A building with a high fire load may still be effectively compartmentalized with doors that can impede the spread of hot smoke and fire gases. Conversely, buildings with open fire plans or unprotected vertical shafts can provide the fire with unrestricted access to fuel throughout the structure.

The contents of a structure represent a readily available source of fuel for a compartment fire. The quantity and nature of the building's contents have a significant influence on fire development. Fuels with a high heat of combustion and heat release rate contribute to a more intense and rapidly developing fire. For instance, synthetic furnishings like polyurethane foam can undergo rapid pyrolysis under fire conditions, even when located at a distance from the fire's origin, thus accelerating the progression of the fire.

The type of construction materials used in a building also impacts the fuel load. Certain building materials, such as wood, are inherently combustible and can contribute to the availability of fuel. In wood frame buildings, not only the structural members but also combustible interior finishes like wood paneling can play a significant role in fire spread. Understanding the combustibility of construction materials is essential in assessing the potential fuel load and the rate at which a fire can spread within a structure.

The proximity and continuity of contents and structural fuels play a significant role in fire development. The location of these fuels in relation to the fire can greatly impact the speed and extent of fire spread. For example, fuels located in the upper levels of adjacent compartments will be more rapidly subjected to the heat of the hot gas layer, leading to faster pyrolysis and involvement in the fire. Continuous fuels, such as combustible interior finishes, can quickly facilitate the spread of fire from one compartment to another.

Additionally, the specific location of the fire within the building can also influence fire development. When a fire originates in the lower levels of a building, such as the basement or first floor, convected heat will cause vertical extension through unprotected stairways and vertical shafts. This vertical extension can contribute to the rapid spread of fire to upper levels. In contrast, fires that originate on upper levels generally exhibit slower downward progression.

COMPARTMENT VOLUME AND CEILING HEIGHT

The volume of a compartment and its ceiling height are factors that significantly impact fire development. In general, larger compartments require more heat energy to raise the temperature of the increased volume of air and structural materials. However, it is important to note that a large compartment with a greater volume of air can support the development of a larger fire before ventilation becomes a limiting factor.

A high ceiling in a compartment can create a deceptive situation where the extent of fire development may not be immediately apparent. This is because the high ceiling allows a large volume of hot smoke and other fire gases to accumulate at the ceiling level, while conditions at the floor level may remain relatively unchanged. This situation is particularly dangerous because if the hot gas layer at the ceiling ignites, conditions can rapidly escalate and become extremely hazardous.

VENTILATION

Ventilation plays a crucial role in the development of a fire within a compartment. The existing ventilation in a structure, which includes structural openings, construction type, and building ventilation systems, has a significant impact. Buildings naturally exchange air with the outside through openings such as windows, doors, and cracks. Additionally, heating, ventilating, and air conditioning (HVAC) systems contribute to air exchange.

When analyzing fire development, it is essential to consider the potential openings that can alter the ventilation profile under fire conditions. For instance, windows can fail or doors may be left open, leading to increased ventilation. When a fire reaches a state where it becomes ventilation controlled, the available air supply becomes a determining factor in the speed, extent, and even the direction of fire development.

THERMAL PROPERTIES OF THE ENCLOSURE

Well-insulated compartments minimize heat loss, allowing more heat to be retained within the space and increasing the temperature, which in turn accelerates the combustion reaction. Surfaces that reflect heat back into the compartment contribute to the intensification of the fire. Materials like masonry act as heat sinks, retaining heat energy and sustaining high temperatures for extended periods. On the other hand, materials such as steel have high thermal conductivity, readily transferring heat to other combustible materials through conduction, potentially spreading the fire beyond the initially involved compartment.

Thermal windows, specifically those with multiple panes, can also contribute to fire development by containing heat within the compartment. The multiple panes of thermal windows create a barrier that restricts the dissipation of heat, potentially causing the fire to grow more rapidly within the enclosed space.

AMBIENT CONDITIONS

Ambient conditions, including temperature, humidity, and wind, can affect fire development in different ways. While ambient temperature and humidity may have limited direct impact within a structure due to its design, they can still influence the ignitability of certain fuels. However, their effects are generally less significant compared to other factors.

High humidity and cold temperatures inside a structure typically have minimal impact on fire development. However, they can affect the movement of smoke, making it less buoyant and potentially hindering its natural flow and dispersion.

On the other hand, wind can be a crucial factor in fire behavior, both in outdoor and indoor settings. Strong winds can greatly influence the spread and intensity of a fire, particularly when ventilation conditions change. For example, if a window fails or a door is opened on the windward side of a building, the increased air supply caused by the wind can lead to a significant increase in fire intensity and rapid fire spread.

Fire control theory

Firefighters control and extinguish fires by disrupting one or more of the essential elements required for combustion (represented by the fire tetrahedron). They achieve this by implementing strategies to reduce temperature, eliminate or isolate the fuel source, alter the oxygen concentration, or interrupt the self-sustaining chemical chain reaction. By actively intervening in these ways, firefighters are able to influence fire behavior and bring the fire under control.

TEMPERATURE REDUCTION

One of the primary methods used to control and extinguish fires is through the application of water for cooling. By reducing the temperature of the fuel, the production of flammable vapors can be diminished, leading to the suppression of the fire. This approach is particularly effective for solid fuels and liquid fuels with high flash points. Water is also highly effective in extinguishing smoldering fires. To successfully reduce the temperature and extinguish the fire, sufficient water must be applied to absorb the heat generated by combustion. However, it's important to note that cooling with water may not be sufficient to extinguish fires involving low flash point flammable liquids and gases. Different types of streams and extinguishing methods will be discussed later in the manual.

In addition to its cooling properties, water can be utilized to control burning gases and lower the temperature of hot combustion products located above the neutral plane. This helps to slow down the process of pyrolysis and reduces the potential for extreme fire behavior, such as flashover.

Water exhibits a significant heat absorption capability as it is heated, but its most powerful effect occurs when it vaporizes into steam. When water undergoes this phase change at 212ºF (100ºC), it expands approximately 1,700 times in volume. This expansion rate highlights the importance of proper nozzle techniques, utilizing an appropriate volume of water, and applying water in the most effective form (such as fog, straight stream, or solid stream) based on the existing fire conditions. Excessive steam production can hinder visibility and increase the risk of steam burns.

FUEL REMOVAL

The most effective way to extinguish a fire is by removing the fuel source. Allowing the fire to burn until all the fuel is consumed is a straightforward method of fuel removal. While it may not always be the most desirable approach, there are situations where it is appropriate. For instance, fires involving pesticides or flammable liquid spills may cause significant environmental harm if extinguished with water, leading to substantial runoff. In such cases, it may be better to let the fire burn, minimizing the pollution of groundwater.

Another way to remove the fuel source is by halting the flow of liquid or gaseous fuel. This can be achieved by closing a valve or by eliminating solid fuels that are in the path of the fire. This method is particularly suitable for extinguishing pressurized gas fires.

OXYGEN EXCLUSION

Limiting the availability of oxygen is an effective method to reduce the growth of a fire and potentially extinguish it. A common example of this is when a cover is placed on a pan of burning grease to smother a rangetop fire. In situations where oxygen needs to be displaced, flooding an area with an inert gas like carbon dioxide disrupts the combustion process by removing oxygen. Another method involves using foam to blanket certain fuels, effectively separating them from oxygen. It's important to note that these methods may not work on self-oxidizing fuels, which have their own oxygen source.

While restricting ventilation is not typically used for extinguishing structure fires, it can be a highly effective strategy for controlling fires. A simple example is when a building occupant closes the door to a room on fire before evacuating. This action limits the air supply to the fire and can help prevent flashover. Similarly, firefighters can control the air supply during firefighting operations by avoiding the opening of doors and windows until fire control has been achieved. This helps limit fire growth and enhances overall fire control efforts.

CHEMICAL FLAME INHIBITION

Certain extinguishing agents, such as certain types of dry chemicals, halogenated agents (halons), and their replacements, are capable of interrupting the combustion reaction and extinguishing flames. This method of extinguishment is particularly effective on gas and liquid fuels since they require a flame to sustain combustion. However, these agents may not be as effective in extinguishing surface fires, as they primarily target the chemical chain reaction involved in flaming combustion.

Special hazards

The industrial workplace presents specific fire hazards due to the presence of various materials and processes. These hazards include electrical ignition sources as well as the use of flammable and combustible liquids and gases, which can create significant fire risks. It is crucial to incorporate the proper installation and maintenance of electrical equipment into any fire prevention program.

Within the workplace, there are several common and hazardous materials that pose fire risks. These include flammable and combustible liquids, liquefied petroleum gases, hydrogen gas, oxygen, and acetylene. To effectively manage these fuel and oxidizer sources, it is essential to adhere to proper handling and storage requirements. Additionally, implementing work procedures that focus on housekeeping and controlling ignition sources is integral to a comprehensive fire protection program.

ELECTRICITY AS AN IGNITION SOURCE

In the United States, approximately thirty thousand fires occur annually, and investigations have revealed that a significant number of these fires originate from electrical sources. Common causes of electrical-initiated fires include short circuits, ground faults, and other electrical failures. The causes of fires in industrial and manufacturing facilities reflect the diverse range of industrial processes and activities carried out. Among these structures, 39 percent of fires were attributed to various equipment and processes categorized as "other equipment." Open flames, embers, or torches ranked second, followed by electrical distribution equipment in third place. Effective industrial fire prevention strategies must address the specific processes and hazards associated with each activity.

Within the workplace, there are multiple electrical sources that can contribute to fires. Examples of these sources include production equipment, electrical wiring, and heating equipment, among others. The diagram provided illustrates typical electrical hazards found in a worksite. It is essential for all electrical installations to adhere to the National and other applicable standards.

Electrical fires in the workplace can arise from various electrical problems. Improper equipment usage, incorrect installation, and inadequate equipment maintenance are among the common causes of electrical fires. Here are examples of sources that can lead to electrical fires in the workplace:

- Improper use of electric cords: This includes running cords under rugs, over nails, or through high traffic areas, as well as using extension cords as a permanent wiring solution.

- Lack of maintenance: Failing to implement a preventive maintenance program to identify and address potential issues before they escalate.

- Ground failure: Neglecting to maintain a continuous path to ground, which can expose electrical systems to damage and pose hazards to workers using unprotected equipment.

- Damaged insulation: Over time, insulation protecting current-carrying wires can become compromised, resulting in exposed wires. When the exposed hot and neutral wires come into contact, a short circuit can occur, serving as an ignition source for fires.

- Sparking: Friction sparking occurs when two hard surfaces, one of which is metal, collide, creating mechanical heat.

- Circuit overload: Overloading a circuit happens when there are more appliances connected to it than it can safely handle. As a result, the wiring overheats, leading to blown fuses or tripped circuit breakers.

- Short circuit: A short circuit occurs when a bare hot wire comes into contact with a bare neutral wire or a grounded wire (or any other ground). The excess current flow results in blown fuses or tripped circuit breakers.

- Arcing: Arcing happens when an electric circuit carrying current is intentionally or unintentionally interrupted.

By addressing these potential issues and implementing proper electrical safety practices, the risk of electrical fires in the workplace can be significantly reduced.

HAZARDOUS LOCATIONS AND THE NATIONAL ELECTRICAL CODE

The placement of electrical equipment in certain environments can introduce a fire hazard. Environments that contain high concentrations of flammable vapors, ignitable fibers, or combustible dusts have the potential to ignite if exposed to electrical equipment and installations. To prevent the ignition of flammable and combustible vapors by electrical wiring and equipment, it is essential for all electrical components used in hazardous locations to adhere to appropriate design requirements.

The National Electrical Code (NEC) provides classifications for different locations based on the potential presence of hazardous materials in the atmosphere. These classifications help determine the specific design specifications that electrical equipment must meet to minimize the risk of fire and explosion hazards. By following these design guidelines, the potential for electrical equipment to act as an ignition source is reduced, and enhancing overall safety in hazardous environments.

Class I locations

Class I locations refer to areas where flammable gases or vapors are present or may be present in the air in quantities that can potentially form explosive or ignitable mixtures.

Class I, Division 2 locations are specific areas characterized by the following conditions:

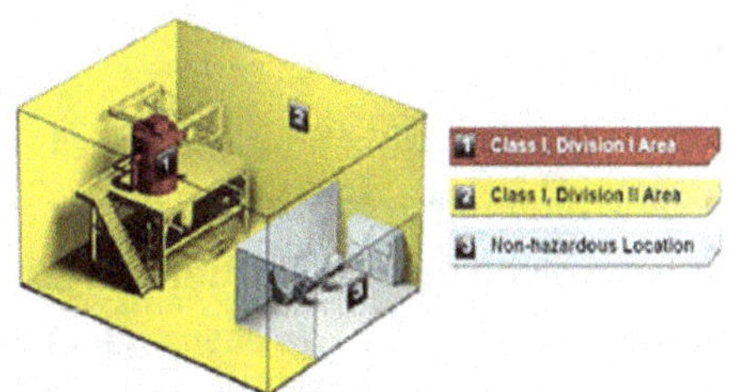

1. The handling, processing, or use of volatile flammable liquids or flammable gases occurs. However, these liquids, vapors, or gases are typically contained within closed systems or containers. The potential for their release exists only in the event of accidental rupture or malfunction of the equipment or systems, or during abnormal operation.

2. Normally, the presence of ignitable concentrations of gases or vapors is prevented through effective mechanical ventilation. However, there is a possibility of such concentrations becoming hazardous if there is a failure or abnormal operation of the ventilation equipment.

3. The location is in close proximity to a Class I, Division 1 area. Occasionally, ignitable concentrations of gases or vapors may be communicated to this area, unless adequate positive pressure ventilation is implemented to ensure a supply of clean air and effective safeguards are in place to prevent ventilation failure.

Class II locations

Class II locations are designated as hazardous due to the presence of combustible dust. A Class II, Division I location can meet any of the following criteria:

1. Under normal operating conditions, there is an adequate amount of combustible dust present to form explosive or ignitable mixtures.

2. The mechanical malfunction or abnormal operation of machinery or equipment could generate such explosive or ignitable mixtures. This can also create potential ignition sources through simultaneous failures of electrical equipment, operation of protective devices, or other causes.

3. Combustible dust with inherent electrical properties may be present in quantities that pose a hazard.

Class II, Division 2 locations exhibit the following conditions:

1. Combustible dust is typically not present in the air in quantities sufficient to form explosive or ignitable mixtures. Dust accumulations are generally minimal and do not impede the normal operation of electrical equipment or other apparatuses. However, there may be instances of dust suspension in the air due to occasional malfunctions of handling or processing equipment.

2. Accumulations of combustible dust on, in, or near electrical equipment may hinder the safe dissipation of heat from the equipment or become ignitable in the event of abnormal operation or equipment failure.

Class III locations

Class III locations are considered hazardous due to the presence of easily ignitable fibers or flyings. However, these fibers or flyings are not typically in suspension in the air in quantities sufficient to form ignitable mixtures.

Class III, Division I locations are specific areas where ignitable fibers or materials that produce combustible flyings are handled, manufactured, or used. Examples of such locations include certain sections of textile mills, plants involved in manufacturing and processing combustible fibers, clothing manufacturing facilities, and woodworking plants. The easily ignitable fibers and flyings found in these locations can include materials like rayon, cotton (including cotton linters and cotton waste), jute, and hemp.

On the other hand, Class III, Division 2 locations are areas where easily ignitable fibers are stored or handled, excluding those involved in the manufacturing process. These locations primarily deal with the storage or handling of these fibers rather than their active production.

SAFE DESIGN OF ELECTRICAL EQUIPMENT

The selection of equipment for use in hazardous locations is based on the characteristics of the flammable vapors, liquids, gases, combustible dusts, or fibers that may be present in those environments, as well as the likelihood of the presence of a flammable or combustible concentration or quantity.

Intrinsic safety is a protection concept employed in potentially explosive atmospheres. It involves designing electrical apparatus in such a way that it cannot release enough energy, either thermally or electrically, to cause ignition of a flammable gas. When equipment is specifically designed for hazardous environments and meets intrinsic safety criteria, it is considered intrinsically safe.

For equipment, wiring methods, and installations in hazardous (classified) locations, there are three options:

1. Equipment and associated wiring approved as intrinsically safe can be used in any hazardous (classified) location for which it is approved.

2. Equipment must be approved not only for the class of location but also for the specific properties of the gas, vapor, dust, or fiber that will be present, in terms of their ignitability or combustibility.

3. Equipment must be appropriately marked according to applicable electrical codes.

The equipment used in a hazardous location should be of a type and design that the employer can demonstrate will provide protection from the hazards associated with the combustibility and flammability of vapors, liquids, gases, dusts, or fibers.

In Division 2 locations, equipment that has been approved for a Division 1 location of the same class and group may be installed. However, general-purpose equipment or equipment in general-purpose enclosures can be installed in Division 2 locations if it does not pose a source of ignition under normal operating conditions.

FLAMMABLE LIQUIDS AND COMBUSTIBLE LIQUIDS

Flammable and combustible liquids present a distinct hazard in the workplace due to their ability to fuel a fire and their relatively low ignition temperature. These liquids are categorized as either flammable or combustible based on their flash point. The flash point refers to the minimum temperature at which a liquid produces vapor in a test vessel at a concentration sufficient to form an ignitable mixture with air near the liquid's surface. During a fire involving flammable or combustible liquids, it is the vapor above the liquid's surface that burns. Liquids with lower flash points have a higher likelihood of generating a sufficient vapor concentration at lower temperatures.

Flammable liquids

Flammable liquids are defined as liquids with a flash point below 100ºF (38°C), except for mixtures where the components with flash points of 100ºF (38ºC) or higher make up 99 percent or more of the total volume. In general, at normal room temperature, flammable liquids can produce vapors that are sufficient to ignite without the need for external heating. Flammable liquids are categorized as Class I liquids and are further divided into three classes:

1. Class IA includes liquids with flash points below 73ºF (23ºC) and boiling points below 100ºF (38°C).

2. Class IB includes liquids with flash points below 73ºF (23ºC) and boiling points at or above 100ºF (38°C).

3. Class IC includes liquids with flash points at or above 73ºF (23ºC) and below 100ºF (38°C).

Combustible liquids

Combustible liquids typically require external heating to generate a sufficient concentration of vapors for ignition.

Combustible liquids are classified into two classes.

Class II liquids include those with flash points at or above 100ºF (38ºC) and below 140ºF (60ºC), except for mixtures where the components with flash points of 200ºF (93ºC) or higher make up 99 percent or more of the total volume.

Class III liquids include those with flash points at or above 140ºF (60ºC). Class III liquids are further divided into two subclasses:

1. Class IIIA liquids include those with flash points at or above 140ºF (60ºC) and below 200ºF (93ºC), except for mixtures where the components with flash points of 200ºF (93ºC) or higher make up 99 percent or more of the total volume of the mixture.

2. Class IIIB liquids include those with flash points at or above 200ºF (93ºC).

UPPER AND LOWER EXPLOSIVE LIMITS

As previously mentioned, for a flammable liquid to ignite, it needs to release enough vapors at its surface in a concentrated form. When the temperature is below the flash point, the liquid evaporates slowly, resulting in insufficient vapor generation. The presence of flammable or combustible vapors in the air determines whether a combustible concentration exists. If the vapor concentration in the air is too low, there won't be enough vapors to ignite, referred to as being below the lower flammable limit (LFL) or lower explosive limit (LEL). This condition is often described as "too lean" in terms of vapors.

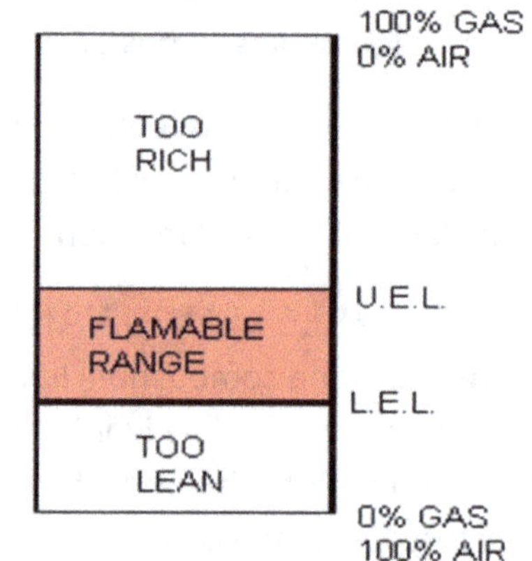

Conversely, if the vapor concentration in the air is above the upper flammable limit (UFL) or upper explosive limit (UEL), the vapors will not ignite. This is commonly known as the vapors being "too rich." Hence, for combustion to occur, flammable and combustible vapors must be present in concentrations above the LFL or LEL but below the UFL or UEL in the air.

FLAMMABLE AND COMBUSTIBLE LIQUID STORAGE

Flammable and combustible liquids can be stored in various ways within the workplace. There are several storage methods available, including portable-container storage, tank storage, storage cabinets, and storage rooms. These options provide different levels of containment and protection for the liquids, allowing for safe storage in accordance with the applicable regulations and standards.

CONTAINERS AND PORTABLE TANKS

In industrial settings, it is common practice to store flammable and combustible liquids in containers. A container refers to any can, barrel, or drum. Barrels typically have a capacity of 42 gallons, while safety cans are approved containers with a maximum capacity of 5 gallons. Safety cans are equipped with a spring-closing lid and spout cover, designed to release internal pressure in case of heat exposure. Drums can hold up to 60 gallons, while tanks have a capacity exceeding 60 gallons. It is important to note that barrels, safety cans, drums, and tanks used in the workplace must be approved for such use by a Nationally Recognized Testing Laboratory. This ensures compliance with safety standards and regulations.

TRANSFERRING FLAMMABLE AND COMBUSTIBLE LIQUIDS

Liquids

In industrial settings, it is common to transfer flammable and combustible liquids from one storage container to another. This task poses various hazards, including potential liquid spills, release of vapors into the work area, and the risk of accidental ignition. To ensure safety, flammable liquids must always be stored in approved, covered containers when not in use. In areas where these liquids are used or handled, appropriate measures should be in place to promptly and safely dispose of any leakage or spills, except in closed containers.

To prevent the ignition of vapors, it is essential to avoid using Class I liquids in the presence of open flames or other potential sources of ignition along the vapor path. When transferring flammable or combustible liquids within a building, it is recommended to use a closed-piping system or devices that draw the liquid from safety cans through the top. Gravity transfer through an approved self-closing valve is another safe option. Transferring liquids by applying air pressure to the container or portable tank is prohibited due to the associated risks.

It is crucial to take adequate precautions to prevent the ignition of flammable vapors. Potential sources of ignition include open flames, lightning, smoking, cutting and welding operations, hot surfaces, frictional heat, static, electrical and mechanical sparks, spontaneous ignition from heat-producing chemical reactions, and radiant heat. Given the high fire hazard of Class I liquids, it is advisable to use a bonding wire to interconnect the nozzle and container during dispensing into containers. Alternatively, a metallic floor plate can be used while the fill stem is connected to the container. When transferring Class I liquids inside buildings, it is important to ensure adequate ventilation to prevent the accumulation of flammable vapors in hazardous concentrations. If mechanical ventilation is necessary, it should remain operational during the transfer process to maintain a safe environment.

STORAGE CABINETS

Storage cabinets are widely utilized for the storage of flammable and combustible liquids contained in drums, barrels, and containers. The primary purpose of these cabinets is to safeguard the stored liquids and, in the event of heat exposure, limit the internal temperature to a maximum of 325ºF. They are constructed to withstand a ten-minute fire test and possess various features for enhanced safety.

Storage cabinets are typically constructed using steel materials, ensuring durability and fire resistance. They are equipped with self-closing doors, which aid in preventing the spread of fire. In cases where it is required by code, cabinets are also designed with ventilation systems to direct any potentially hazardous vapors to the outside. Moreover, the cabinets are raised at least 2 inches above the cabinet's bottom to prevent direct contact between the stored liquids and the floor.

For compliance with safety standards, it is essential that storage cabinets are approved for the storage of flammable and combustible liquids, meeting the design and construction guidelines outlined by the National Fire Protection Standards Agency of the respective country. These cabinets should be clearly labeled with conspicuous lettering stating "Flammable – Keep Flame Away," indicating the potential hazards associated with the stored contents. By adhering to these specifications, the storage cabinets contribute to maintaining a secure environment for the storage of flammable and combustible liquids.

INSIDE STORAGE ROOM

Storage rooms utilized for the specific purpose of storing flammable and combustible liquids in industrial settings must be meticulously designed and constructed to ensure safe storage practices. Several key design elements should be considered, including fire protection, spill containment, ventilation, fire resistance, and proper electrical wiring and equipment.

To prevent the unintentional spread of spilled flammable or combustible liquids from the storage room to other areas of the facility, measures should be taken to protect openings such as doorways. Additionally, it is crucial to ensure that the room is constructed in a manner that creates a liquid-tight seal where the walls meet the floor.

Fire protection within the storage room is achieved through the presence of fire extinguishers. As per general workplace regulations, there should be at least one portable fire extinguisher, rated at a minimum of 12-B units, located outside but within 10 feet of the storage room's door opening. If the storage area contains Class I or Class II liquids, an additional fire extinguisher meeting the same requirements must be positioned no less than 10 feet but no more than 25 feet away from any storage area located outside the storage room but within the same building. Open flames and smoking are strictly prohibited in flammable- or combustible-liquid storage areas.

Factors such as the fire-rating construction of the room and the presence of a sprinkler system are considered when determining these maximum quantities. It is also required to maintain at least one clear aisle, measuring at least 3 feet wide, within the storage room to allow for easy access. Stacking containers with a capacity exceeding 30 gallons one on top of another is prohibited.

Proper ventilation is essential in storage rooms to maintain flammable and combustible vapors below their lower explosive limits (LELs). Ventilation systems should provide a minimum of six air changes per hour throughout the entire volume of the room. In cases where gravity ventilation is implemented, the intake for fresh air and the exhaust outlet should be situated on the exterior of the building housing the storage room.

STORAGE TANKS

Storage tanks are categorized based on their operating pressures and fall into three classifications: low-pressure tanks, atmospheric tanks, and pressure vessels.

- Atmospheric tanks are designed to operate at pressures ranging from atmospheric pressure up to 0.5 pounds per square inch gauge (psig).
- Low-pressure tanks are constructed to withstand pressures above 0.5 psig but not exceeding 15 psig.
- Pressure vessels are designed to handle pressures higher than 15 psig.

When storing flammable and combustible liquids, tanks must be constructed using approved materials such as steel, ensuring compatibility with the stored liquids. The design and construction of these tanks should adhere to recognized standards. Furthermore, the safety requirements for storage tanks can be further classified based on whether they are intended for above-ground or underground use.

OUTSIDE ABOVEGROUND TANKS

To control and prevent fires involving above-ground storage tanks, various methods can be employed, including tank separation, diking and drainage systems, and proper venting. These measures help minimize fire spread, provide access during emergencies, and regulate pressure changes within the tanks.

Tank separation involves maintaining a minimum distance between storage tanks to limit the potential spread of fire. Factors considered when determining the required separation include tank diameters, capacities, and the characteristics of the stored liquids. The following criteria are commonly used:

• The minimum distance between any two flammable or combustible liquid storage tanks should not be less than 3 feet (1 meter).

• The distance between adjacent tanks should be at least one-sixth the sum of their diameters.

Venting is essential for maintaining a consistent pressure inside storage tanks, compensating for temperature changes and liquid displacement. However, venting can also pose fire hazards if flammable or combustible vapors escape through the vent piping and come into contact with an ignition source.

Emergency relief venting is another crucial aspect, ensuring that excessive internal pressure caused by fires is safely relieved. Different pressure-relieving constructions, such as floating roofs, lifter roofs, or weak roof-to-shell seams, can be employed. Design capacities should be met to prevent tank rupture. Commercial tank-venting devices should be labeled with information such as the opening pressure, full open position pressure, and flow capacity in cubic feet per hour of air at 60ºF and 14.7 psia.

Drainage and diking systems help prevent accidental liquid discharge into adjacent properties, waterways, or surrounding areas. Requirements for diking and drainage include:

1. Drainage systems should direct liquid to vacant land, designated areas, or an impounding basin with a capacity equal to or larger than the largest tank being served.

2. Diked areas should have sufficient volumetric capacity to contain the maximum amount of liquid that could be released from the largest tank within the enclosure.

Implementing these measures ensures safer storage of flammable and combustible liquids in above-ground tanks, reducing the risk of fires and environmental contamination.

UNDERGROUND TANKS

Underground storage tanks that contain flammable and combustible liquids present both fire and environmental hazards. Proper placement and construction of these tanks are crucial to mitigate risks. Here are important considerations for underground storage tanks:

1. Placement: Tanks should be installed in areas free from potential hazards caused by excessive loads from buildings and vehicle traffic. Care should be taken during handling to avoid damaging the tank, breaking welds, puncturing, or scraping off protective coatings. Tanks should be surrounded by noncorrosive and inert backfill material such as clean sand, earth, or gravel, properly compacted in place.

2. Distance Requirements: To minimize the potential impact of leaks, tanks storing Class I liquids should be positioned at least 3 feet away from any basement or pit wall. For tanks storing Class II or Class III liquids, the minimum distance from any basement, pit, or property line should be 1 foot.

3. Corrosion Protection: Underground storage tanks and their piping must have corrosion protection to prevent leaks and deterioration. This can be achieved through the following methods:

    -   Protective coatings or wrappings

    -   Cathodic protection, which utilizes sacrificial anodes or impressed current systems to prevent corrosion

    -   Use of corrosion-resistant construction materials

4. Ventilation: Similar to above-ground tanks, underground storage tanks require proper venting to maintain appropriate internal pressure during filling and emptying operations.

Implementing these measures helps ensure the safe and reliable storage of flammable and combustible liquids in underground tanks, reducing the risks of leaks, fires, and environmental contamination. Regular inspections and maintenance are also essential to detect and address any potential issues promptly.

TANK VEHICLE AND TANK CAR LOADING AND UNLOADING

The transfer of flammable and combustible liquids from tank vehicles and tank cars carries similar hazards as transferring liquids between portable containers. These hazards include the presence of flammable vapors and the risk of static-electrical ignition. To ensure safety and protect adjacent property, loading and unloading facilities for Class I liquids should be located no closer than 25 feet to adjacent property, while facilities for Class II and Class III liquids should maintain a minimum distance of 15 feet.

Equipment used for transferring liquids from tank cars and rail cars must be approved for the specific class of liquid being handled. To prevent spills and overfilling, approved valves that are self-closing or automatically shut off when the vehicle is full or reaches a certain level should be utilized.

During the transfer process, there can be a potential difference in electrical potential between the tank car or truck and the receiving tank. Similar to transferring between containers, bonding should be implemented to equalize the electrical potential. When loading Class I liquids or Class II and III liquids into vehicles that may contain vapors from previous cargoes of Class I liquids, bonding should be established. This involves connecting a metallic bond wire between the fill stem, rack structure, or any metallic part in electrical contact with the cargo tank vehicle. The bonding connection is made prior to raising dome covers and should remain in place until the filling process is complete and all dome covers are closed and secured.

By adhering to these safety practices, the transfer of flammable and combustible liquids from tank vehicles and tank cars can be conducted with reduced risks of spills, ignition, and other hazards.

Workplace practices

In order to safeguard employees and property from fire hazards related to flammable and combustible liquids in the workplace, it is crucial to implement and adhere to control measures and workplace procedures. Compliance with regulations set by OSHA, NFPA, and other relevant organizations is essential for the safe storage and handling of these liquids. These regulations outline specific guidelines for housekeeping, fire protection, and the management of ignition sources. By following these procedures, the risk of fire incidents can be effectively controlled.

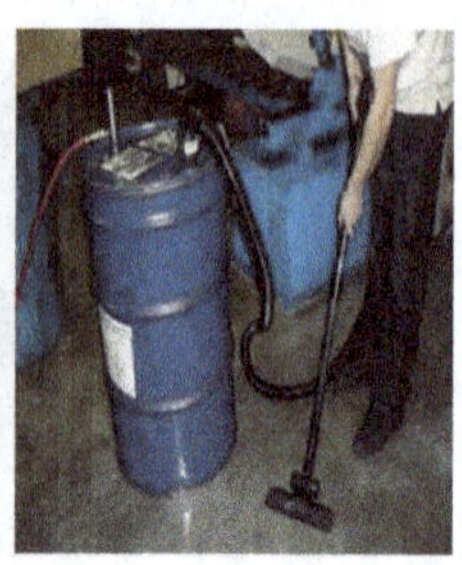

CONTROLLING SOURCES OF IGNITION

When dealing with areas where flammable vapors are present, it is vital to take necessary precautions to prevent ignition by effectively eliminating or controlling potential sources of ignition. Such sources can include open flames, lightning, smoking, cutting and welding activities, hot surfaces, frictional heat, sparks (both static, electrical, and mechanical), spontaneous ignition, chemical and physical-chemical reactions, as well as radiant heat. By actively addressing and managing these sources, the risk of ignition and subsequent fire incidents can be significantly reduced.

MAINTENANCE AND REPAIRS

Prior to conducting maintenance work in an area where flammable or combustible liquids are processed, it is crucial to obtain authorization from a responsible representative of the employer. Specifically, hot work activities such as welding or cutting operations, the use of power tools that generate sparks, and chipping operations should only be permitted under the supervision of a designated individual who is in charge of ensuring safety. This responsible individual must conduct a thorough inspection of the work area to ensure its safety and confirm that appropriate procedures will be followed for the specified maintenance work. These measures are necessary to minimize the risk of accidents or incidents related to the presence of flammable or combustible liquids during maintenance operations.

HOUSEKEEPING

Adherence to established procedures is essential for maintaining safe maintenance and operating practices in relation to flammable or combustible liquids. These procedures aim to control leaks, prevent accidental releases of such liquids, and promote prompt cleanup of spills. It is important to maintain adequate aisles in order to ensure unobstructed movement of personnel and allow fire protection equipment to access all areas of the storage room effectively.

To minimize fire hazards, combustible waste material and residues within buildings or operating areas should be kept to a minimum. They should be stored in covered metal receptacles and disposed of on a daily basis.

Effective housekeeping practices also involve the removal of dust accumulations within the premises. By promptly removing dust, the risk of secondary dust explosions and potential ignition sources can be reduced. Implementing efficient dust-extraction systems in areas prone to dust accumulation is recommended. Dust should be promptly removed using either a high-power explosion-proof vacuum cleaner or an internal vacuuming system that directs the dust to a central collection system. These measures contribute to maintaining a safe environment and preventing fire incidents.

Hydrogen

Hydrogen, although nontoxic and colorless, possesses certain inherent risks due to its flammability and potential for explosive mixtures with air. It lacks odor, making it difficult to detect without proper monitoring. When combined with oxidizers like air, oxygen, or halogens, hydrogen can react violently. Moreover, hydrogen can displace oxygen in the atmosphere, leading to asphyxiation risks if present in high concentrations.

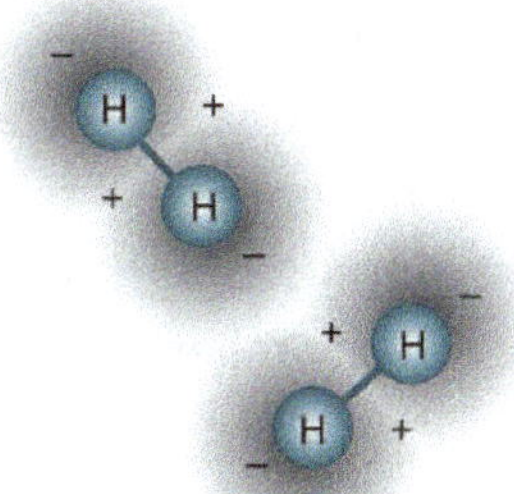

Various industries utilize hydrogen for its diverse applications. It can be stored in containers such as cylinders or be part of a larger system involving tanks, piping, and manifolds. Hydrogen may exist in its gaseous form or be stored under pressure as a liquefied substance. Regardless of the storage state, it is crucial to strictly adhere to safety standards governing the storage and handling of hydrogen in the workplace.

Containers used for storing hydrogen, whether cylinders or tanks, must conform to relevant design and construction requirements. These standards ensure the integrity and safety of the containers to minimize the risks associated with hydrogen storage.

Each portable container and manifolded hydrogen supply unit should be clearly labeled with the name "HYDROGEN" for easy identification. The storage area for hydrogen must have permanent placards prominently displayed, indicating the presence of flammable gas. The placards should bear the inscription "HYDROGEN - FLAMMABLE GAS _ NO SMOKING_ NO OPEN FLAMES" or an equivalent warning message.

To minimize the risk of accidental ignition, systems containing hydrogen should be positioned above ground level and situated away from potential sources of ignition. These potential sources may include electric power lines, flammable-liquid piping, or other piping carrying flammable gases. The preferred location for a hydrogen storage facility is determined based on the following order of preference, as indicated by Roman numerals in the following table:

Maximum capacities of Gaseous Hydrogen Systems

Natural of Location	Size of Hydrogen System		
	Less than 3,000 CF	3,000-15,000 CF	More than 15,000 CF
Outdoors	I	I	I
In a separate building	II	II	II
In a special room	III	III	Not permitted
Inside buildings, not in a special room, and exposed to other occupancies	IV	Not permitted	Not permitted

LIQUEFIED HYDROGEN SYSTEMS

Proper storage and handling of liquefied hydrogen in the workplace is crucial to prevent fire hazards. Liquefied hydrogen is obtained by compressing and cooling hydrogen to -250°C, and it retains many of the hazards associated with its gaseous state. Therefore, any containers used to store liquefied hydrogen must be designed, constructed, and tested according to the appropriate standards, such as the ASME Boiler and Pressure Vessel Code, Section VIII-Unfired Pressure Vessels (1968), or applicable provisions of API Standard 620, Recommended Rules for Design and Construction of Large, Welded, Low-Pressure storage Tanks. The following guidelines should be followed to ensure safe storage and handling of liquefied hydrogen in the workplace.

1. Portable containers used for storing liquefied hydrogen should be designed, constructed, and tested according to the specifications and regulations set by the U.S. Department of Transportation (USDOT).
2. The containers must be clearly marked with the label "LIQUEFIED HYDROGEN - FLAMMABLE GAS" for easy identification.
3. Safety relief devices should be installed on the containers as required by applicable regulations to prevent excessive pressure buildup.
4. Piping, tubing, fittings, gaskets, and thread sealants used in the system should be suitable for hydrogen service, capable of withstanding the pressures and temperatures involved, and in compliance with relevant standards.
5. Valves, gauges, regulators, and other accessories used in the liquefied hydrogen system should be specifically designed for such service and appropriate for the pressures and temperatures encountered.
6. Electrical wiring and equipment within a 3-foot radius of regularly made and disconnected connections must meet the requirements for Class I, Group B, Division 1 locations. These locations are characterized by the presence of flammable gases or vapors under normal operating conditions.
7. Electrical wiring and equipment within 25 feet of regularly made and disconnected connections or within 25 feet of a liquid-hydrogen storage container should adhere to the standards outlined in Subpart S of the OSHA (Occupational Safety and Health Administration) regulations for Class I, Group B, Division 2 locations. These locations involve the potential for the presence of flammable gases or vapors under abnormal operating conditions.

The storage of liquefied hydrogen in the workplace should adhere to specific guidelines to ensure safety. The location of the storage area, determined by the maximum quantity of liquefied hydrogen, should follow the order of preference indicated by Roman numerals in Table 3.5. For portable containers with a capacity of 50 gallons or less, housed inside buildings without a special room and exposed to other occupancies, the following minimum requirements must be met:

1. Maintain a distance of 20 feet from flammable liquids and easily combustible materials like excelsior or paper.
2. Keep a distance of 25 feet from ordinary electrical equipment and other potential ignition sources, including process or analytical equipment.
3. Ensure a distance of 25 feet from concentrations of people.
4. Maintain a distance of 50 feet from the intakes of ventilation and air-conditioning equipment or compressors.
5. Keep a distance of 50 feet from storage areas containing other flammable gases or oxidizing gases.

Containers storing liquefied hydrogen should be protected against damage or injury from falling objects or work activities in the area. They should be securely fastened and stored in an upright position. Welding, cutting operations, and smoking must be strictly prohibited in the vicinity while hydrogen is present. Similar to the storage of hydrogen gas, storage of liquefied hydrogen must comply with requirements for construction and location of storage buildings, venting, noncombustible construction materials, electrical wiring, ventilation, and explosion venting.

ACETYLENE

Acetylene is commonly used as a fuel in welding and cutting operations, and is stored in cylinders or tanks. Its high solubility in acetone allows for large quantities to be stored at low pressures. The composition of acetylene is 92.3 percent carbon and 7.7 percent hydrogen, and it produces a much higher flame temperature than other fuels. The gas is actually produced from liquid acetone stored in an inert filler material inside the cylinder. Tipping the cylinder can cause the release of liquid acetone.

When using acetylene cylinders for oxy-acetylene welding and cutting, the acetylene serves as the fuel and the oxygen as the oxidizer. One hazard is the potential for fires since the fuel and oxidizer are stored together. Separating the fuel and oxygen cylinders by a distance of 20 feet can help reduce this risk. It is important to always store acetylene cylinders in an upright position since they rely on the liquid acetone inside the container.

OXYGEN

Oxygen is a nonflammable gas that serves as an oxidizer in fires, supporting combustion. When in contact with greases and oils, pure oxygen can cause spontaneous combustion. Therefore, it is crucial to clean equipment in a bulk oxygen system to remove any oil, grease, or other readily oxidizable materials before putting the system into service.

Oxygen can be stored in cylinders or in bulk. A bulk oxygen system consists of various equipment, including storage containers, pressure regulators, safety devices, vaporizers, manifolds, and interconnecting piping. If the system has a storage capacity of more than 13,000 cubic feet of oxygen at normal temperature and pressure (NTP) and is connected in service or ready for service, or if it has a capacity of more than 25,000 cubic feet of oxygen (at NTP) including unconnected reserves on site, it is considered a bulk oxygen system.

Bulk oxygen systems must adhere to applicable codes during design and installation. Here are some provisions related to bulk oxygen systems:

1. Bulk oxygen storage systems should be located outdoors above ground or installed in a building with noncombustible construction. They must be adequately vented and used exclusively for oxygen storage.
2. The chosen location should ensure that containers and associated equipment are not exposed to electric power lines, flammable or combustible liquid lines, or flammable gas lines.
3. A minimum safe distance must be maintained between any bulk oxygen storage container and potential exposures, such as combustible structures, fire-resistive structures, wall openings, combustible liquid storage, and combustible gas storage.
4. High-pressure gaseous-oxygen containers must comply with applicable codes, including the ASME Boiler and Pressure Vessel Code, Section VIII - Unfired Pressure Vessels, and USDOT specifications and regulations.
5. Piping, tubing, and fittings should be suitable for oxygen service, considering the pressures and temperatures involved. They should conform to the "Gas and Air Piping Systems" Code for Pressure Piping, ANSI B31.1-1967, with addendum B31.10a-1969.
6. All bulk oxygen storage containers, regardless of design pressure, must be equipped with safety relief devices as required by the ASME code or USDOT specifications and regulations.
7. Bulk oxygen storage containers designed and constructed according to the ASME Boiler and Pressure Vessel Code, Section VIII - Unfired Pressure Vessel, should have safety relief devices that meet the

provisions of the Compressed Gas Association Pamphlet Safety Relief Device Standards for Compressed Gas Storage Containers, S-1, Part 3.

Valves, gauges, regulators, and other accessories used in bulk oxygen systems must be suitable for oxygen service. Enclosures containing oxygen control or operating equipment should be adequately vented. The bulk oxygen storage location should be permanently placarded with signs indicating "OXYGEN - NO SMOKING - NO OPEN FLAMES" or an equivalent warning.

LIQUEFIED PETROLEUM GAS

Liquefied petroleum (LP) gas finds diverse applications in industries, such as fuel for heating processes, power source for equipment like powered industrial trucks and vehicles, and propellant in aerosol products. However, it is crucial to implement control measures due to the highly flammable nature of LP gas. These measures include the use of approved equipment for storage and transfer, control of ignition sources, and proper handling procedures. LP gas is typically stored in portable cylinders or as part of a fixed industrial process in a manifold system.

LP gas stored in containers regulated by the United States Department of Transportation (USDOT) must be equipped with approved valves, connectors, manifold valve assemblies, and regulators. The design, construction, and testing of containers should comply with the appropriate regulations, such as the Rules for Construction of Unfired Pressure Vessels of the ASME Boiler and Pressure Vessel Code. Containers filled based on volume should have a fixed liquid-level gauge to indicate the maximum permitted filling level.

Any welding, repairs, or modifications performed on LP gas containers should follow approved methods to minimize the potential for fires and explosions. LP gas containers must be labeled with a metal nameplate securely attached to the container in a visible manner even after installation. The nameplate should provide the following information:

1. Name and address of the container supplier or the trade name of the container.
2. Water capacity of the container in pounds or gallons (U.S. Standard).
3. Design pressure of the container in pounds per square inch gauge (psig).
4. Statement: "This container shall not contain a product having a vapor pressure in excess of ___ psig at 38°C (100ºF)."
5. Tare weight of the container in pounds or another identified unit of weight (for containers with a water capacity of 300 pounds or less).
6. Maximum filling level of the container for temperatures ranging between -7°C (20ºF) and 54°C (130ºF) (except for containers with fixed maximum-level indicators or filled by weight), marked in increments of no more than -7°C (20ºF). This marking may be located on the liquid-level gauging device.
7. Outside surface area of the container in square feet.

Each individual container shall be located with respect to the nearest important building or group of buildings as follows (measurement is water capacity per container):

Less than 125 gallons	underground- 10 feet	aboveground- none
125 to 250 gallons	underground- 10 feet	aboveground- 10 feet
251 to 500 gallons	underground- 10 feet	aboveground- 10 feet
501 to 2,000 gallons	underground- 25 feet	aboveground- 25 feet
2,001 to 30,000 gallons	underground- 50 feet	aboveground- 50 feet
30,001 to 70,000 gallons	underground- 50 feet	aboveground- 75 feet
70,001 to 90,000 gallons	underground- 50 feet	aboveground- 100 feet

Fire Extinguishment

Fires require four elements to sustain: fuel, oxygen, heat, and a chain reaction. These components can be targeted to extinguish a fire. By removing any one of the four elements, a fire can be eliminated. Firefighters use various methods to attack one or more of the fire tetrahedron's components and put out a fire. Firefighting equipment can range from portable fire extinguishers to fixed sprinkler systems to fire hoses that spray water or steam.

PORTABLE FIRE EXTINGUISHERS

Portable fire extinguishers are commonly used fire protection devices found in homes, businesses, and fire apparatus. They are designed to be used on small fires in their early stages. In many situations, a portable extinguisher can quickly control or extinguish a small fire, saving valuable time compared to deploying a larger hose line. Some fire departments assign a team member equipped with a water-type or multipurpose portable extinguisher during initial attack on high-rise fires. If the fire remains small, the extinguisher can be used to put out the fire effectively.

It is crucial to understand the different types of portable fire extinguishers, their capabilities, limitations, and safe applications. This knowledge allows for proper selection and use of extinguishers. This section provides information on the various types of portable fire extinguishers, their ratings, inspection procedures, and guidelines for selection and use.

TYPES OF PORTABLE FIRE EXTINGUISHERS

There is a wide variety of portable fire extinguishers available, each with its own operational characteristics. The table below outlines the properties of different types of portable fire extinguishers discussed in the following subsections. These extinguishers employ at least one of the following mechanisms to extinguish fires:

- Smothering: These extinguishers work by excluding oxygen from the fire, effectively smothering it.

- Cooling: These extinguishers reduce the temperature of the burning material below its ignition point, extinguishing the fire.

- Chain breaking: These extinguishers disrupt the chemical chain reaction occurring during combustion, halting the fire.

- Saponification: These extinguishers create a soapy foam that excludes oxygen, smothering the fire.

The following table presents the operational characteristics of different types of portable fire extinguishers:

Type of Extinguisher	Mechanism	Operational Characteristics
Water	Cooling	Effective against Class A fires (ordinary combustibles)
Foam	Smothering, Cooling	Effective against Class A and B fires (flammable liquids)
Carbon Dioxide (CO_2)	Smothering	Effective against Class B and C fires (flammable liquids and electrical fires)
Dry Chemical	Smothering, Chain Breaking	Effective against Class A, B, and C fires
Wet Chemical	Saponification	Effective against Class K fires (cooking oil and fat fires)

Extinguisher	Type	Agent	Fire Class	Size	Stream Reach	Discharge time
Pump-Tank Water	Hand-carried backpack	water	A only	1 ½-5 gal (6 L to 20 L)	30-40 ft	45sec to 30 min
Stored-pressure water	Hand-carried	water	A only	1 ¼-21/2 gal (5 L to 10 L)	30-40ft(9.1m to 12.2m)	30-60 sec
Aqueous Film Forming Foam(AFFF)	Hand-carried	water and AFFF	A & B	2 ½ gal (10 L)	20-25 ft (6.1m to 7.6m)	Approximately 50 sec
Halon 1211	Hand-carried wheeled	halon	B & C	Hand-carried 2 ½-20 lb (1kg to 9 kg) Wheeled: to 150 lb (68 kg)	8-18 ft (2.4m to 5.5m) 20-35ft (6.1m to 10.7m)	8-18 sec 30-44 sec
Halon 1301	hand-carried	halon	B & C	2 ½ lb (1 kg)	4-6 ft (1.2m to 1.8m)	8-10 sec
Clean Agent	Hand-carried	FE- 36™	A, B & C	1.4 to 15.5 lb (.6 kg to 7 kg)	6-18 ft (1.8m to 5.5m)	9-14 sec
Carbon dioxide	Hand-carried	Carbon-dioxide	B & C	2 ½-20 lb (1 kg to 9 kg)	3-8 ft (1m to 2.4m)	8-30 sec
Carbon dioxide	Wheeled	Carbon dioxide	B & C	50-100 lb (23 kg to 45 kg)	8-10 ft (2.4m to 3 m)	26-65 sec
Dry chemical	Hand-carried Stored-pressure Cartridge-operated	Sodium bicarbonate, potassium bicarbonate, ammonium phosphate, potassium chloride	B & C	2 ½- 30lb (1 kg to 14 kg)	5-20 ft (1.5m to 6.1m)	8-25 sec
Multipurpose Dry chemical	Hand-carried stored-pressure	Monoammonium phosphate	A, B & C	2 ½- 30 lb (1 ka to 14 kg)	5-20 ft (1.5m to 6.1m)	8-25 sec

	Cartridge-operated					
Dry chemical	Wheeled: ordinary or multipurpose		A, B & C	75-350 lb (34 kg to 159 kg)	Up to 45 ft (13.7m)	20 sec to 2 min
Dry powder	Hand-carried wheeled	Various, depending on metal fuel	D only	Hand carried: to 30 lb (14kg) Wheeled: 150 lb & 350 lb (68 kg & 159 kg)	4-6 ft (1.2m to 1.8m)	28-30 sec
Wet chemical	Hand-carried	Potassium acetate	K only	2.5 gal (9.5 L)	8-12 ft (2.4m to 3.6m)	75-85 sec

Extinguishing Agent Characteristics

Agent	Primary Mode	Secondary Mode
Water	Cooling	Oxygen depletion
Carbon dioxide	Oxygen depletion	Cooling
Foam	Oxygen depletion	Vapor Suppression
clean Agent	Chain inhibition	Cooling
Dry Chemical	Chain inhibition	Oxygen depletion
Wet Chemical	Oxygen depletion	Vapor Suppression
Dry Chemical	Oxygen depletion	Heat transfer cooling

It is not recommended for firefighters to depend on privately owned fire extinguishers found In buildings. These extinguishers may not be functional due to poor maintenance, vandalism, or obsolescence. Instead, firefighters should rely on the extinguishers carried on their fire apparatus. Pumping apparatus must carry two approved portable fire extinguishers with mounting brackets that are suitable for use on Class B and Class C fires. For a dry-chemical extinguisher, the minimum rating required is 80 B;C. For a carbon dioxide (CO2) extinguisher, the minimum rating required is 10 B:C. The rating system for fire extinguishers denotes the type of fire and its performance capability (refer to the Extinguisher Rating System section). Also pumping apparatus must carry at least one 2 1/2-gallon (10L) or larger water extinguisher that can be used on Class A fires.

Aqueous Film Forming Foam (AFFF) Extinguishers

Aqueous film-forming foam (AFFF) extinguishers are effective for tackling Class A and Class B fires. They are especially useful for extinguishing fires or suppressing vapors from small liquid fuel spills.

AFFF extinguishers differ from stored-pressure water extinguishers in two key aspects. Firstly, the tanks of AFFF extinguishers contain a specific quantity of AFFF concentrate that is mixed with water. Additionally, they feature an air-aspirating nozzle that aerates the foam solution, resulting in higher-quality foam compared to a standard nozzle.

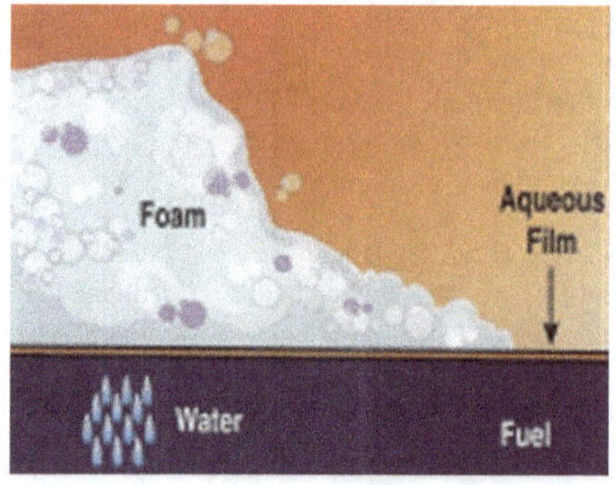

The water/AFFF solution is expelled from the extinguisher by utilizing compressed air or nitrogen stored in the tank along with the solution. When applying the foam, it is important to avoid disturbing the foam blanket directly onto the fuel. Instead, the foam should either gently rain down onto the fuel surface or deflect off an object to ensure its effectiveness.

Carbon Dioxide Extinguishers

Portable carbon dioxide (CO2) fire extinguishers are available in both handheld and wheeled units. They are highly effective for extinguishing Class B and Class C fires. Due to their discharge in the form of gas, they have limited reach, and the gas can be dispersed by wind. These extinguishers do not require freeze protection.

Carbon dioxide is stored in the extinguisher under its own pressure as a liquefied gas, ready to be released when needed. The agent is discharged through a plastic or rubber horn attached to either a short hose or tube.

Wheeled carbon dioxide units are similar to handheld units but much larger in size. They are commonly used in airports and industrial facilities. When responding to a fire, the wheeled unit is brought to the scene, and the hose, typically less than 15 feet (5 meters) in length, needs to be deployed or unwound from the unit before use. The principle of operation remains the same as in the smaller handheld units.

Dry Chemical Extinguishers

Dry chemical agents and dry powder agents are often confused, but they are used for different types of fires. Dry chemical agents are suitable for Class A-B-C fires and/or Class B-C fires, while dry powder agents are specifically used for Class D fires. Dry chemical extinguishers, which contain dry chemical agents, are widely used as portable fire extinguishers. There are two main types: regular B:C-rated and multipurpose A:B:C-rated extinguishers. The characteristics and operation of these types are generally the same, unless stated otherwise.

Commonly used dry chemical agents include sodium bicarbonate, potassium bicarbonate, urea-potassium bicarbonate, potassium chloride, and monoammonium phosphate. These agents are mixed with small amounts of additives during manufacture to make them

moisture-resistant and prevent caking. This ensures that the agents remain ready for use even after long periods of storage and allows them to flow freely.

It's important to note that some dry chemical agents are not compatible with foam. Certain agents, such as monoammonium phosphate and some sodium bicarbonate agents, can disrupt the foam blanket when used in conjunction with foam or applied after foam.

The dry chemical agents themselves are generally considered nontoxic and safe to use. However, the cloud of chemicals they create during discharge can reduce visibility and potentially cause respiratory issues, similar to any airborne particulate. Some dry chemical agents are compatible with foam, while others can degrade the foam blanket. When applying dry chemical agents to Class A fires, the discharge should be directed at the burning material to cover it with the chemical. Once the flames are extinguished, the agent should be intermittently applied to any remaining smoldering hot spots. It's worth noting that many dry chemical agents are corrosive to metals, so it may be more appropriate to use a different agent, such as carbon dioxide, on metal fires.

Extinguishers and Agents for Metal Fires

When it comes to Class D fires involving combustible metals, the previously discussed extinguishing agents are ineffective. Special extinguishing agents and application techniques have been developed specifically for controlling and extinguishing metal fires. It's important to note that no single agent can effectively extinguish fires in all types of combustible metals. Some agents are effective against fires in multiple metals, while others are only effective for specific metals. Additionally, certain powdered agents can be applied using portable extinguishers, while others require the use of a shovel or scoop. The manufacturer's technical sales literature provides detailed information on the appropriate application techniques for specific dry powders.

Portable extinguishers designed for Class D fires are available in both handheld and wheeled models. Regardless of the type of dry powder being used, it must be applied in a sufficient depth to completely cover the burning area and create a smothering blanket. It's important to apply the agent gently to avoid breaking any crust that may have formed over the burning metal, as breaking the crust could cause the fire to flare up and expose more uninvolved material to combustion. Care should also be taken to avoid scattering the burning metal. Additional applications may be necessary to cover any hot spots that develop during the firefighting operation.

In cases where a small amount of burning metal is present on a combustible surface, the fire should first be covered with powder. Then, a layer of powder measuring 1 to 2 inches (25 mm to 50 mm) deep should be spread nearby, and the burning metal should be carefully shoveled onto this layer. Additional powder should be added as needed. After the fire has been extinguished, the material should be left undisturbed until it has cooled completely. Only then should disposal be attempted to ensure safety.

Portable Fire Extinguisher Rating System

Class A Ratings:

Class A portable fire extinguishers are assigned ratings ranging from 1-A through 40-A. The rating for water extinguishers is based on the quantity of extinguishing agent, as well as the discharge duration and range used during testing. For example, a 1-A rating requires 1 ¼ gallons (5L) of water, while a 2-A rating requires 2 ½ gallons (10L) or twice the capacity of a 1-A extinguisher. These ratings are determined through testing with different sizes of fuel cribs.

Class B Ratings:

Extinguishers suitable for Class B fires are given numerical ratings from 1-B through 640-B. The rating is based on the approximate area of a flammable liquid fire, measured in square feet or square meters that a non-expert operator can extinguish. The expectation is that the operator can extinguish 1 square foot (0.09 m2) of fire per numerical rating of the extinguisher.

Class C Ratings:

Class C ratings do not involve specific fire extinguishing capability tests. Since electricity does not burn, extinguishers for Class C fires receive this letter rating because Class C fires are essentially Class A or Class B fires involving energized electrical equipment. The extinguishing agent is tested for electrical non-conductivity. The Class C rating is assigned in addition to the rating for Class A and/or Class B fires.

Class D Ratings:

Class D ratings for extinguishers vary depending on the type of combustible metal being tested. Several factors are considered during testing, including the reaction between the metal and the agent, toxicity of the agent and fumes produced, as well as the time it takes for the metal to burn out with or without fire suppression efforts. Class D agents do not receive numerical ratings and are specific to combating fires involving combustible metals. They cannot be used for other classes of fire.

Class K Ratings:

Extinguishers with Class K ratings are suitable for fires involving kitchen oils such as vegetable oil, peanut oil, canola oil, and other oils with low or no fatty acids. Wet chemical agents containing alkaline mixtures like potassium acetate, potassium carbonate, or potassium citrate are used to saponify the fats or fatty acids, suppressing vapors and smothering the fire. An extinguisher with a Class K rating should be able to extinguish a fire from a deep fryer using light oil with a surface area of 2.25 square feet (0.2m2) or more.

Multiple Markings

Extinguishers suitable for multiple classes of fire are marked with combinations of the letters A, B, and/or C along with the corresponding symbols for each class. Common combinations include Class A-B-C, Class A-B, and Class B-C. It is mandatory for all new portable fire extinguishers to be labeled correctly. Extinguishers without proper markings are not certified units and should not be used.

The ratings for each class of fire on a multi-class extinguisher are independent of each other and do not affect one another. To understand the rating system better, consider a common-sized multipurpose extinguisher with a rating of 4-A 20-B:C. This extinguisher should be able to extinguish a Class A fire that is four times larger than a fire rated as 1-A, approximately twenty times as much Class B fire as a 1-B extinguisher, and it should be capable of extinguishing a deep-layer flammable liquid fire with an area of 20 square feet (1.8m2). Additionally, it must be nonconductive to safely use on fires involving energized electrical equipment.

Portable fire extinguishers are identified using two systems. The first system employs geometric shapes of specific colors, with the class letter displayed within the shape. The second system, utilizes pictographs to facilitate the selection of the most appropriate fire extinguisher. It also indicates the types of fires on which the extinguishers should not be used. It is crucial that the markings on the extinguishers are clearly visible for easy identification.

SELECTING AND USING PORTABLE FIRE EXTINGUISHERS

Once a small fire has been detected and the initial steps have been taken, the next course of action is to select the appropriate portable fire extinguisher and use it effectively. Several factors should be taken into account when choosing the right extinguisher for the situation, and there are important guidelines to follow during its use. The following section addresses these considerations in detail.

SELECTING THE PROPER FIRE EXTINGUISHER

Selection of the proper portable fire extinguisher depends on numerous factors.

- Classification of the burning fuel
- Rating of the extinguisher
- Hazards to be protected
- Size and intensity of the fire
- Atmospheric conditions
- Any life hazard or operational concerns
- Ease of handling extinguisher
- Availability of trained personnel

USING PORTABLE FIRE EXTINGUISHERS

Portable fire extinguishers are available in a variety of sizes and types. While the operational procedures for each type are similar, it is important for firefighters to familiarize themselves with the detailed instructions provided on the extinguisher label. Regular inspections of fire extinguishers on emergency response vehicles are necessary to ensure accessibility and functionality.

Before using any fire extinguisher in an emergency, a quick check should be conducted. This check is crucial to verify that the extinguisher is charged and operational, as it can protect against injuries caused by a defective or depleted extinguisher. If the extinguisher appears to be in proper working order, it can be utilized to suppress the fire.

During the inspection prior to use, the following should be checked:

- External condition: Ensure there is no visible damage to the extinguisher, indicating its structural integrity.
- Hose/nozzle: Confirm that the hose or nozzle is securely in place, as it is essential for the proper discharge of the extinguishing agent.
- Weight: Assess the weight of the extinguisher, ensuring it feels as though it contains the appropriate amount of extinguishing agent.
- Pressure gauge (if available): If the extinguisher is equipped with a pressure gauge, check that the needle indicates an operable range, indicating sufficient internal pressure.

Once the appropriate size and type of extinguisher have been selected for the situation, approach the fire from the windward side. This means positioning oneself with the wind at the back. This approach helps prevent the fire, smoke, or airborne particles from blowing directly into the face, enhancing visibility and ensuring a safer firefighting operation.

PASS METHOD OF APPLICATION

All modern fire extinguishers are operated in a similar manner, eliminating the need for inversion. After performing the quick check mentioned earlier, grasp the extinguisher by its handle and carry it to the location where it will be used. To suppress the fire effectively, follow the PASS method:

P - Pull the pin, breaking the thin wire or plastic seal.

A - Aim the nozzle directly at the source of the fire.

S - Squeeze the handles together to release the extinguishing agent.

S - Sweep the nozzle back and forth to cover the burning materials.

Ensure that the extinguishing agent reaches the fire, as it would be wasted otherwise. Keep in mind that smaller extinguishers may require closer proximity to the fire compared to larger units. Radiant heat or adverse winds can limit the reach of the extinguishing agent.

Operating the extinguisher close to the fire can sometimes scatter lightweight solid fuels or penetrate the surface of liquid fuels. Apply the agent from a point where it reaches the fire without disturbing the fuel. Releasing the handle will stop the flow of the agent.

After the fire has been suppressed, it may be necessary to move closer for final extinguishment. If a single extinguisher does not achieve complete extinguishment, reassess the situation and withdraw if needed. For solid fuel in the smoldering phase, appropriate tools can be used to overhaul and separate the fuel, followed by soaking it with a charged hoseline for complete extinguishment. In the case of a liquid fuel fire, applying the appropriate type of foam through a hoseline or using multiple extinguishers simultaneously may be necessary.

If multiple extinguishers are being used simultaneously, coordinate with other firefighters and maintain awareness of each other's actions and positions. After use, place empty fire extinguishers on their sides. This indicates that they are empty and reduces the risk of someone mistakenly using an empty extinguisher during an emergency.

INSPECTING PORTABLE FIRE EXTINGUISHERS

Most fire codes require annual inspections of portable fire extinguishers to ensure their accessibility and functionality. It is essential to verify that extinguishers are in their designated locations, unactivated, untampered with, and free from obvious physical damage that may hinder their operation. Property owners or building occupants are responsible for the servicing of portable fire extinguishers and other fire suppression or detection equipment they own.

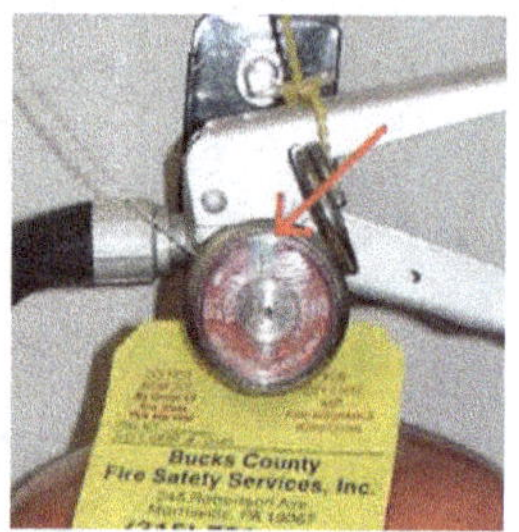

Firefighters should also include extinguisher inspections as part of their building inspection program, although it is typically performed by the building owner or their representative. When conducting these inspections, remember that three factors determine the value of a fire extinguisher: its serviceability, accessibility, and simplicity of operation.

Guidelines for hydrostatic testing of extinguisher cylinders, and test results must be affixed to the extinguisher shell. High-pressure and low-pressure cylinders have different recording methods for hydrostatic test results.

Maintenance personnel should consult proper regulations and guidelines for specific information on extinguisher testing and documentation.

The following procedures should be followed during every fire extinguisher inspection:

- Ensure the extinguisher is in the correct location and easily accessible.
- Inspect the discharge nozzle or horn for obstructions, cracks, and dirt or grease accumulations.
- Check the extinguisher shell for any physical damage.
- Verify that the operating instructions on the extinguisher nameplate are legible.
- Inspect the locking pin and tamper seal to ensure the extinguisher has not been discharged or tampered with.
- Determine if the extinguisher is full of agent and fully pressurized by checking the pressure gauge, weighing the extinguisher, or inspecting the agent level. If the extinguisher is found to be deficient in weight by 10 percent, it should be taken out of service and replaced.
- Review the inspection tag for the date of the previous inspection, maintenance, or recharging.
- Examine the condition of the hose and its fittings.

If any of the above items are deficient, remove the extinguisher from service and repair it according to department policies. Replace the extinguisher with one that has an equal or greater rating.

Sprinkler Systems

Sprinkler systems are designed to provide fire protection by automatically distributing water onto a fire to extinguish it or control its spread until firefighters arrive. These systems consist of a series of sprinklers, also known as sprinkler heads, strategically placed throughout the building. Water is supplied to the sprinklers through a network of pipes, which can be either exposed or hidden within the walls or ceilings.

There are two main types of sprinkler coverage: complete sprinkler coverage and partial sprinkler coverage. A complete sprinkler system covers the entire building, ensuring comprehensive fire protection. On the other hand, a partial sprinkler system only protects specific areas, such as high-hazard areas, exit routes, or locations specified by fire codes or the authority having jurisdiction.

It is crucial that the automatic sprinkler system and all its component parts are listed and approved by nationally recognized testing laboratories like Underwriters Laboratories Inc. or FM Global. Automatic sprinkler systems are considered the most reliable fire protection devices. Firefighters need to have a solid understanding of the basic system and the operation of pipes and valves. It is also important for firefighters to be familiar with the various applications of sprinkler systems and how they impact life safety in different scenarios.

In rare cases where automatic sprinkler systems fail to operate, it is usually not due to the failure of the sprinklers themselves. Reports indicate that sprinkler systems may not perform properly due to various reasons, including:

- Partially or completely closed main water control valve: If the main water control valve of the sprinkler system is closed, it will prevent water from reaching the sprinklers, rendering them ineffective.
- Interruption to the municipal water supply: If there is a disruption or loss of water supply from the municipal source, the sprinkler system may not have the necessary water pressure to operate correctly.
- Damaged or painted-over sprinklers: Sprinklers that are damaged, obstructed, or painted over may not release water properly during a fire, limiting their effectiveness.
- Frozen or broken pipes: Freezing temperatures can cause pipes to freeze and potentially burst, leading to a loss of water flow in the sprinkler system.
- Excess debris or sediment in the pipes: Build-up of debris or sediment in the pipes can restrict water flow and hinder the sprinkler system's ability to function optimally.
- Failure of a secondary water supply: Some sprinkler systems may rely on secondary water sources, such as tanks or pumps. If these secondary systems fail or are not adequately maintained, the sprinkler system may be compromised.
- Tampering and vandalism: Deliberate tampering or vandalism of the sprinkler system, such as damaging sprinkler heads or obstructing them, can prevent proper operation during a fire event.
- Sprinklers obstructed by objects stacked too closely: If objects or materials are stacked too close to sprinkler heads, it can obstruct the water spray pattern and impede the system's ability to control or extinguish a fire.

Effects of Sprinkler Systems on Life Safety

The presence of a sprinkler system enhances the safety of building occupants by quickly discharging water onto a fire when it is still in its early stages. This rapid response helps to extinguish or control the fire before it can grow larger, limiting the production of harmful combustion products. Sprinklers are particularly effective in the following situations:

1. Preventing fire spread upwards in multistory buildings: Sprinkler systems are designed to suppress fires in their early stages, preventing the upward spread of flames and reducing the risk of fire escalation in tall buildings.
2. Protecting the lives of occupants in other parts of the building: By containing or extinguishing fires, sprinkler systems help to create safer conditions for occupants in areas of the building not directly affected by the fire. This allows occupants to evacuate more safely or seek refuge in designated safe areas until help arrives.

However, there are situations where sprinklers alone may not be as effective, including:

1. Fires that are too small to activate the sprinkler system: Sprinklers are typically designed to activate when exposed to a certain level of heat. In very small fires that do not generate sufficient heat, the sprinkler system may not activate, requiring alternative fire suppression measures.
2. Smoke generation reaching occupants before the sprinkler system activates: Sprinklers primarily address the fire itself and may not immediately address the generation and spread of smoke. If smoke reaches occupants before the sprinkler system activates, it can hinder visibility and pose respiratory hazards.
3. Occupants who are sleeping, intoxicated, or handicapped: In situations where occupants may have reduced awareness or mobility, such as when they are sleeping, intoxicated, or have disabilities, reliance solely on sprinklers may not provide adequate protection. Additional fire safety measures, such as effective smoke alarms and clear evacuation procedures, are crucial in these cases.

SPRINKLERS

Sprinklers function by releasing water when a heat-responsive element, such as a fusible link, is activated. This element acts as a trigger to open the sprinkler individually in response to heat. Essentially, each sprinkler acts as a fixed-spray nozzle that activates when the surrounding temperature reaches a certain threshold. There are various types and designs of sprinklers available to suit different applications.

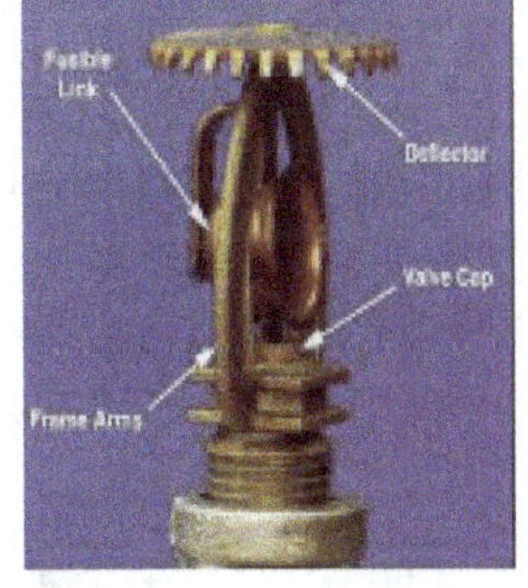

One common way to identify sprinklers is by the temperature at which they are designed to operate. This temperature is typically indicated through color-coding the sprinkler frame arms, using differently colored liquid in bulb-type sprinklers, or stamping the temperature directly onto the sprinkler itself. These markings provide crucial information for understanding the specific temperature range at which each sprinkler is designed to activate.

Three commonly used release mechanisms for activating sprinklers are fusible links, frangible bulbs, and chemical pellets. Each of these mechanisms responds to heat and initiates the sprinkler operation.

Fusible link

A sprinkler with a fusible link consists of a frame attached to the sprinkler piping. Two levers press against the frame and a cap covering the water outlet. The fusible link holds the levers together until the link melts due to the heat of a fire. Once the link melts, water pressure pushes the levers and cap aside, allowing water to flow from the orifice. The water then strikes the deflector attached to the frame, converting it into a spray for efficient fire extinguishment. Quick-response mechanisms using specially designed fusible links have been developed to enhance life safety, allowing for faster sprinkler activation and fire suppression.

Frangible bulb

Some sprinklers incorporate a small bulb filled with liquid and an air bubble that keeps the orifice closed. The air bubble prevents false activations caused by normal temperature fluctuations. In a fire, the heat expands the liquid inside the bulb, absorbing the air bubble. This increases the internal pressure until the bulb shatters at the intended temperature. The breaking temperature is determined by the amount of liquid and the size of the bubble in the bulb. The liquid inside the bulb is color-coded to indicate the designated breaking temperature. When the bulb shatters, it releases the valve cap.

Chemical pellet

A sprinkler with a chemical pellet features a solder pellet under compression within a small cylinder. The pellet melts at a predetermined temperature, allowing a plunger to move down and release the valve cap parts.

The operating temperature of sprinkler heads is typically identified using a color-coded system. The colors may be painted on the arm of a sprinkler head with a fusible link, or the color of the liquid inside a bulb-style sprinkler head indicates its operating temperature.

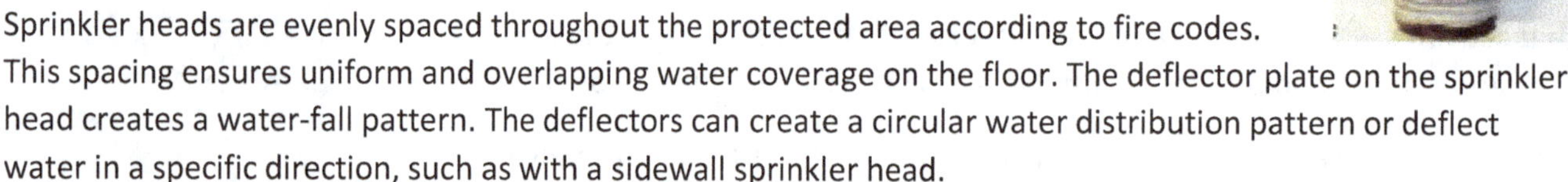

Sprinkler heads are evenly spaced throughout the protected area according to fire codes. This spacing ensures uniform and overlapping water coverage on the floor. The deflector plate on the sprinkler head creates a water-fall pattern. The deflectors can create a circular water distribution pattern or deflect water in a specific direction, such as with a sidewall sprinkler head.

SPRINKLER POSITION

Sprinklers are installed in three primary positions: pendant, upright, and sidewall. Each position is designed to provide a specific spray pattern and coverage. It's important to use sprinklers specifically designed for a particular position and not interchange them with those intended for different positions. Additionally, there are special-purpose sprinklers available for specific applications.

Pendant sprinklers

These are the most commonly used sprinklers and hang down from the underside of the piping. They spray a stream of water downward into a deflector, which breaks the stream into a hemispherical (umbrella-shaped) pattern.

Upright sprinklers

These sprinklers are screwed into the top of the piping and discharge water into a solid deflector. The deflector breaks the water into a hemispherical spray pattern that is redirected toward the floor.

Sidewall sprinklers

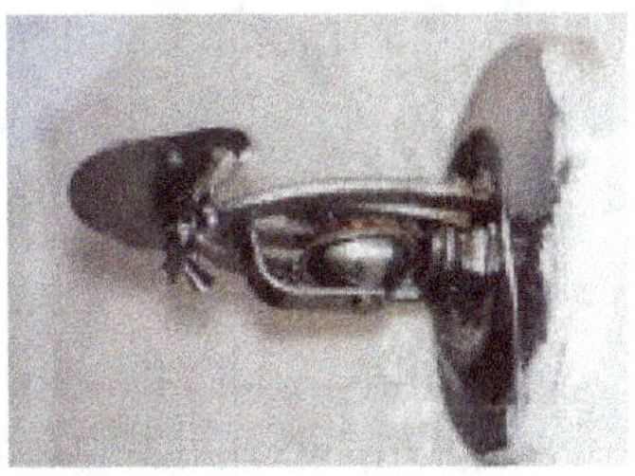

These sprinklers extend from the side of a pipe and are utilized in small rooms where the branch line runs along a wall. They have a special deflector that creates a fan-shaped pattern of water.

Special-purpose sprinklers

These sprinklers are designed for specific applications due to their unique characteristics. For instance, special-purpose sprinklers with corrosive-resistant coatings are intended for installation in areas with corrosive atmospheres. Other special-purpose sprinklers are designed to be recessed in the ceiling to blend in with the room's decor or serve specific purposes in specific environments.

SPRINKLER-SYSTEM TESTS AND INSPECTIONS

Sprinkler systems should undergo regular tests and inspections to ensure their proper functioning and reliability. In addition to the inspector's test, the 2-inch main-drain test, water-flow alarm tests, and fire department-connection tests, the following items should be inspected on a sprinkler system:

1. Test all alarms at least once a year to ensure they are operational and can effectively alert occupants and emergency responders in the event of a fire.

2. Subject all piping to a hydrostatic test to verify its strength and integrity and check for any leaks that may compromise the system's effectiveness.

3. Conduct trip tests, clean and reset dry-pipe valves, and test the antifreeze solution in the system during springtime to ensure proper functionality after the winter season.

4. Inspect the building for insulation problems and potential sources of freezing, as freezing can impair the operation of sprinklers.

5. Regularly inspect sprinklers for corrosion or accumulation of foreign materials. Frequent inspections are necessary to address these issues promptly and prevent any compromise in the sprinkler system's performance.

6. Remove any accumulations of foreign materials, such as paint, from sprinkler heads, as these can interfere with their water discharge capability and potentially raise the temperature at which they activate.

7. Corrosion can severely damage sprinkler heads, rendering them inoperative or weakened. Inspections should identify and address any corrosion issues to ensure the reliability of the sprinkler system.

WATERFLOW ALARMS

Waterflow alarms in sprinkler systems are designed to detect the flow of water through the system, indicating the activation of sprinklers due to a fire. There are two common types of waterflow alarms: hydraulic alarms and electric alarms.

1. Hydraulic Alarms: A hydraulic alarm is a local alarm that operates based on the flow of water through the system. When water flows through the sprinkler system, it activates a water motor, which in turn drives a local alarm gong or bell. The purpose of this alarm is to alert personnel within the building or nearby individuals that the sprinkler system has been activated due to a potential fire. Hydraulic alarms are primarily used for local notification.

2. Electric Alarms: An electric waterflow alarm is an alarm system that utilizes electrical components to detect water flow in the sprinkler system. When water flows through the system, it triggers sensors or switches that send an electrical signal to the alarm panel. The alarm panel can be configured to activate audible and visual alarms within the building, alerting occupants to the potential fire situation. Additionally, electric waterflow alarms can be connected to a monitoring service or directly to the fire department to notify them of the activation and prompt a response.

WATER SUPPLY

The majority of sprinkler systems are designed to have a water supply that meets the necessary requirements in terms of volume, pressure, and reliability. The minimum water supply should be able to deliver the required volume of water to the highest sprinkler in the building while maintaining a residual pressure of at least 15 psi (105 kPa).

The minimum flow of water for the sprinkler system depends on factors such as the specific hazards being protected, the type of occupancy, and the contents of the building. These factors determine the amount of water needed to effectively control or suppress a fire.

A connection to a public water system is often an excellent source of water for automatic sprinkler systems. Public water systems typically have adequate volume, pressure, and reliability to meet the demands of a sprinkler system. In many cases, a connection to the public water system is the primary or only water supply available for the sprinkler system.

In most cases, the water supply for a sprinkler system is designed to provide an adequate flow and pressure to a fraction of the sprinklers installed in the system. This is known as a designed density or area of operation. The idea behind this design approach is to ensure that there is sufficient water supply for a controlled fire, but in the event of a large fire or a pipe breakage, additional water and pressure may be required to effectively suppress the fire.

To provide this additional water and pressure, sprinkler systems are equipped with a fire department connection (FDC). A fire department connection is a connection point on the outside of a building that allows fire department pumpers to supply water to the sprinkler system. It enables the fire department to augment the water supply and pressure in case of a significant fire event.

Typically, fire department connections consist of a siamese connection with two or more 2½-inch (65 mm) female connections. Each connection is equipped with a clapper valve that prevents backflow of water. Alternatively, a single large-diameter connection attached to a clappered inlet may be used. The fire department can connect their pumper apparatus to the FDC and supply additional water and pressure to the sprinkler system, enhancing its effectiveness in controlling or extinguishing the fire.

The fire department pumpers that supply water to the sprinkler system should have a capacity of at least 1,000 gpm (4,000 L/min) or greater. In addition, there should be a minimum of two 2 1/2-inch (65 mm) or larger hoses attached to the FDC to provide the necessary water supply and pressure to the sprinkler system. It is also recommended that fire department pumpers supplying attack lines should operate from hydrant connections to mains other than the main supplying the sprinkler system whenever possible to avoid reducing the water pressure and flow to the sprinkler system.

FIRE HYDRANTS

There are two major types of fire hydrants used in the United States: the dry barrel and the wet barrel hydrants.

1. Dry Barrel Hydrant: The dry barrel hydrant is commonly used in areas where temperatures drop below freezing. It is designed to prevent the water in the hydrant from freezing and causing damage. In a dry barrel hydrant, the valve is located below the frost line to keep it protected from freezing temperatures. A drain valve is present at the base of the hydrant, allowing any residual water in the barrel to drain out, preventing it from freezing and potentially damaging the hydrant.

2. Wet Barrel Hydrant: The wet barrel hydrant, sometimes referred to as the "California" hydrant, is typically used in warmer climates where freezing temperatures are not a concern. This type of hydrant has valves at each outlet, allowing water to be readily available at each connection point. In a wet barrel hydrant, the water is constantly present in the barrel, hence the term "wet." It is important to note that wet barrel hydrants are not suitable for use in freezing conditions as the water inside the hydrant can freeze and cause damage.

STANDPIPE AND HOSE SYSTEMS

A standpipe system is a fire protection system that provides a fire-hose attachment station on each floor of a building. It is designed to transport water for firefighting purposes from a reliable water supply to designated areas of a building. Standpipe systems are an important component of a building's fire safety infrastructure and provide a means for occupants and firefighters to access water quickly during a fire emergency.

The basic components of a standpipe system include:

1. Hose: Fire hoses are stored on hose racks or in hose cabinets on each floor. These hoses can be connected to the standpipe system and used by occupants or firefighters for manual firefighting.

2. Piping: The piping in a standpipe system is typically made of steel to withstand the pressure and provide durability. It is designed to distribute water from the water supply to various hose stations throughout the building.

3. Hose Case or Station: Hose cases or stations are located on each floor and serve as storage for the fire hoses. They are usually equipped with doors or covers to protect the hoses from damage and ensure their readiness for use.

Standpipe systems can be connected to a variety of water sources. In some cases, they are connected to a municipal water supply that is always present and ready for use. However, there are also dry standpipe systems where the fire department needs to connect their water supply to the standpipe system through external connections located outside the building. These dry standpipe systems require the fire department to actively supply water to the system during a fire event.

EXTINGUISHING PROPERTIES OF WATER

Water extinguishes fire primarily by cooling and smothering. When heated, water absorbs heat as it converts into steam through vaporization. This process involves both raising the temperature of the water and changing its state. The visible form of steam is condensed steam.

Heat absorption requires energy to raise the temperature and change the state of a substance. Specific heat refers to the amount of heat energy needed to raise the temperature of a given mass of a substance by one degree. In the SI system, it's measured for 1 gram of a substance increasing by 1°C, while in the customary system, it applies to 1 pound of a substance increasing by 1°F. Latent heat of vaporization is the energy required to convert a substance from a liquid to a gaseous phase.

Complete vaporization of water takes time as the heat must be maintained until the entire volume is vaporized. Breaking water into small droplets, such as with a fog nozzle, increases its surface area exposed to heat. This leads to faster heat absorption and conversion into steam compared to compact streams from small bore nozzles.

For instance, a large ice cube dropped into water takes time to absorb heat because only a small surface area is exposed. However, dividing the ice cube into smaller cubes increases the surface area exposed to water, allowing for faster heat absorption. This principle applies similarly to water in its liquid state.

The effectiveness of different types of nozzles, such as solid streams and fog streams, depends on the specific circumstances of a fire. The solid stream, being more compact, has a smaller surface area and may absorb heat less efficiently compared to a fog stream. However, it is inaccurate to claim that one type of nozzle is superior in all situations.

The key factor in fire suppression is delivering enough water to the fire to absorb the heat being generated. In some cases, a fog stream may be evaporated before reaching the burning fuel, making it ineffective. In such situations, a solid stream may be necessary to reach the core of the fire.

Water also possesses the capability to expand when heated. At its boiling point of 212°F (100°C), water can expand approximately 1,700 times its original volume as it converts to steam. The degree of expansion varies with temperature, meaning that in hotter environments, water expands to even greater volumes of steam. This expansion helps in cooling the compartment by displacing heat and smoke. However, it's important to note that steam can be hazardous, as it can cause severe burn injuries to firefighters and occupants of the building.

The volume of steam generated during fire suppression is closely related to the amount of water used. Here are two examples to demonstrate the effect of steam expansion in a 10- x 20-foot (3m x 6m) compartment with a 10-foot (3m) ceiling, totaling 2,000 cubic feet (57m3). The examples assume a hot gas layer at approximately 500°F (260°C) and utilize a fog nozzle with a flow rate of 150 gallons per minute (600 liters per minute).

In Example 1, the nozzle operator applies water continuously for one minute, discharging and vaporizing 28 cubic feet (0.79 m³) of water. This water expands to approximately 48,000 cubic feet (1,359 m³) of steam. This volume of steam is sufficient to fill a room with dimensions approximately 10 feet (3 m) high, 50 feet (15 m) wide, and 96 feet (29 m) long.

In Example 2, the nozzle operator uses two short pulses of water fog in the hot gas layer. The total amount of water discharged is 0.33 cubic feet (0.009 m³), which expands to approximately 792 cubic feet (22.43 m³) of steam. This volume of steam is less than half the volume of the compartment. The cooling effect of this water application may cause the hot gas layer to contract, potentially leading to a rise in the level of the hot gas layer.

Indeed, effective extinguishment with water often relies on the production of steam. When water is converted into steam, it absorbs a significant amount of heat energy compared to when it is heated to its boiling point. This process of vaporization allows water to remove heat from the fire more efficiently and contribute to its extinguishment.

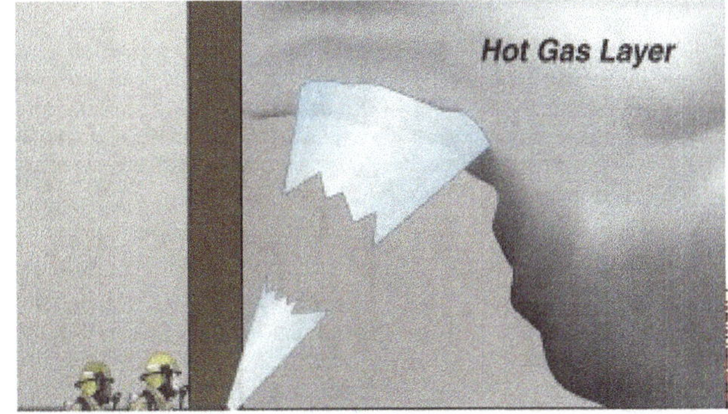

When combating a fire within a compartment, it is crucial to understand the importance of applying water in the correct form and quantity. Skillful nozzle operation, along with coordinated fire attack and ventilation, are essential factors in achieving effective fire control and maintaining a safe working environment.

Proper nozzle techniques ensure that water is delivered to the fire in a manner that maximizes heat absorption and steam production. Coordinated fire attack strategies involve applying water at the right time and location to suppress the fire and prevent its spread. Additionally, ventilation plays a critical role in removing smoke and hot gases, facilitating better visibility and reducing the risk of flashover.

Water is indeed a highly effective extinguishing agent due to its unique characteristics. Here are some key points regarding the valuable properties of water for fire extinguishment:

1. Availability and affordability: Water is widely accessible and is typically inexpensive, making it a practical choice for firefighting purposes.

2. High heat-absorbing capacity: Water has a high specific heat, meaning it can absorb a significant amount of heat energy compared to other commonly used extinguishing agents. This property allows water to cool down the fire and reduce its temperature.

3. Latent heat of vaporization: When water reaches its boiling point and converts into steam, it requires a substantial amount of heat energy. This high latent heat of vaporization enables water to absorb additional heat from the fire, leading to further cooling effects.

4. Versatile application methods: Water can be applied in different forms, including solid stream, fog stream (with variations like straight, narrow, and wide patterns), or broken stream. These application methods offer flexibility in adapting to various fire scenarios and optimizing firefighting effectiveness.

Fire Detection and Alarms

Installing fire detection, alarm, and suppression systems in buildings and properties serves various important purposes. These systems are designed to fulfill specific needs and provide the following functions:

1. Notification and Evacuation: The primary function of these systems is to alert and notify occupants of a facility about the presence of a fire. This allows them to take immediate action and evacuate safely, minimizing the risk to their lives.

2. Summoning Assistance: Fire detection and alarm systems also serve to alert and summon organized assistance, such as the fire department, to initiate or support fire control activities. This helps ensure a timely response and effective firefighting efforts.

3. Automatic Fire Control and Suppression: These systems can automatically activate fire control and suppression measures, such as sprinkler systems or gas-based suppression systems. This helps to contain and extinguish the fire, limiting its spread and damage.

4. Auxiliary Functions: Fire detection and alarm systems can initiate a range of auxiliary functions related to environmental, utility, and process controls. For example, they can activate ventilation systems, shut down machinery, or control elevators to ensure the safety of occupants and facilitate firefighting operations.

Fire detection, alarm, and suppression systems can incorporate one or more of these features, depending on the specific requirements of the property. While these systems can operate mechanically, hydraulically, or pneumatically, modern systems predominantly utilize electronic components for efficient and advanced operation.

TYPES OF ALARM SYSTEMS

The most basic alarm system, known as a protected premises fire alarm system, requires manual initiation by pulling a handle. When activated, these systems alert building occupants to evacuate but do not automatically notify the fire department. Therefore, it is necessary for someone to inform the fire department in case of activation.

Optional features can enhance the capabilities of a local warning system. For instance, automatic fire detection devices can be added to the system to detect the presence of a fire and initiate a signal. These features offer additional protection and are discussed further in the following sections.

There are four main types of automatic alarm-initiating devices designed to detect different aspects of a fire. These include heat detectors, smoke detectors, fire gas detectors, and flame detectors. Each type serves a specific purpose in detecting and signaling the presence of a fire. The following sections provide more detailed information on these commonly used devices.

HEAT DETECTORS

Fixed-Temperature Heat Detectors

Fixed-Temperature Heat Detectors: Fixed-temperature heat detectors are cost-effective and less prone to false activations compared to other types of systems. However, they may be slower to activate in certain situations. These detectors are designed to activate when they reach a specific pre-set temperature. Typically installed on the ceiling, in the highest parts of a room, they respond to heat as it rises. The activation temperature of heat detectors should be slightly higher than the expected ceiling temperatures in the area. Common ratings for living spaces range from 135°F to 174°F (58°C to 79°C), while areas with elevated temperatures may have detectors rated at 200°F (94°C) or higher.

Smoke Detectors/Alarms:

Smoke Detectors: Smoke detectors are devices that detect the presence of smoke or other combustion products. In nonresidential and large multi-family residential occupancies, these devices only detect smoke and transmit a signal to another device that sounds the alarm. These units are called smoke detectors. On the other hand, in single-family residences and smaller multi-family residential occupancies, self-contained units called smoke alarms are used, capable of both detecting smoke and sounding an alarm.

Smoke detectors have an advantage over heat detectors as they can respond to smoke or combustion products at an early stage, even before significant heat is produced. This enables them to initiate an alarm more quickly. Smoke detectors are preferred in many occupancies due to their early detection capabilities. The two main types of smoke detectors are photoelectric and ionization detectors. These are further explained in the following sections, along with information on power sources for smoke alarms.

PHOTOELECTRIC SMOKE DETECTORS

A photoelectric smoke detector, also known as a visible products-of-combustion detector, utilizes a photoelectric cell and a small light source. The photoelectric cell operates in two ways to detect smoke: through beam application and refractory application.

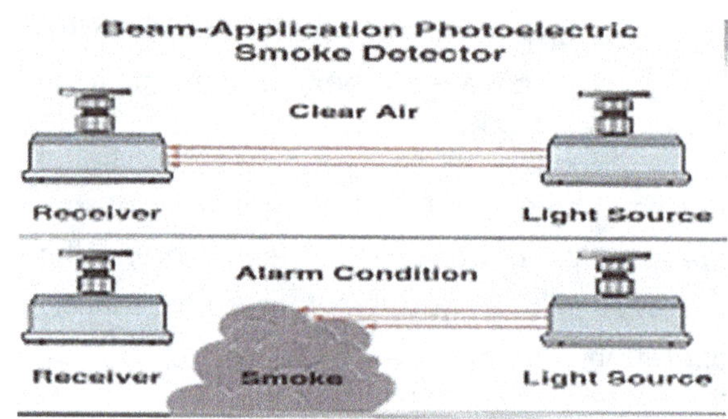

In the beam application type, a light beam is focused across the monitored area onto a photoelectric cell. The cell continuously converts the beam into electrical current, keeping a switch open. When smoke obstructs the path of the light beam, the required amount of current is no longer generated, causing the switch to close and initiate an alarm signal.

The refractory photocell method involves a light beam passing through a small chamber located away from the light source. Under normal conditions, the light does not reach the photocell, resulting in no current and keeping the switch open. However, when smoke enters the chamber, it scatters the light beam in all directions. Some of the scattered light strikes the photocell, creating current flow. This current causes the switch to close and triggers the alarm.

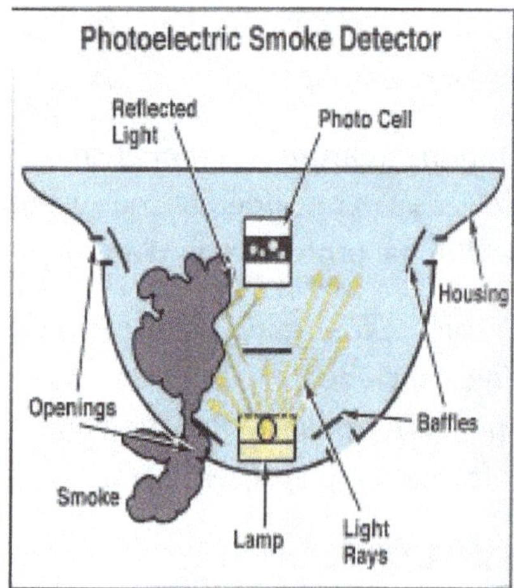

A photoelectric smoke detector effectively functions for all types of fires and automatically resets when the air clears. These detectors are generally more sensitive to smoldering fires compared to ionization detectors.

IONIZATION SMOKE DETECTORS

During the process of combustion, tiny particles and aerosols that are too small to be visible are generated. These unseen products of combustion can be detected by devices that utilize a small quantity of radioactive material, typically americium, to ionize air molecules within a chamber in the detector. The ionized particles enable the flow of electrical current between negative and positive plates present in the chamber. When the particulate products of combustion (smoke) enter the chamber, they attach to the charged air molecules (ions), reducing the conductivity of the air within the chamber. This decrease in current between the plates triggers an alarm signal.

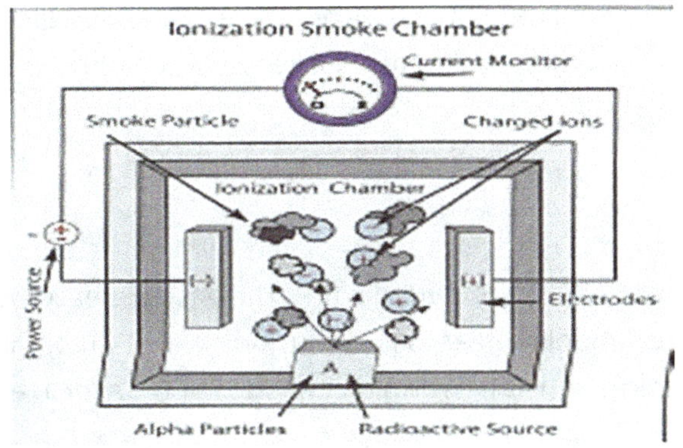

Ionization detectors effectively respond to most fires, although they generally react more quickly to flaming fires compared to smoldering fires. These detectors automatically reset once the air has cleared.

POWER SOURCES

Residential smoke alarms can be powered by either batteries or household current. Battery-operated alarms offer the advantage of easy installation, requiring only a screwdriver and a few minutes. They are independent of house power circuits and can continue to operate during power failures, which is particularly important if the fire is caused by a malfunction in the house wiring. Some newer smoke alarms come with lithium batteries that have a service life of 10 years.

Firefighters should be aware of any local laws regarding smoke alarms, as they may specify the power source and installation requirements for different occupancies, including homes. In some areas, laws may require hard-wired units due to concerns about maintenance issues with battery-operated alarms. Hard-wired alarms powered by household current are generally more reliable. However, in rural areas or areas prone to frequent power failures, battery-operated units may be more dependable.

It is crucial to use the specific type of battery recommended by the alarm's manufacturer for replacements. The batteries should be changed at least twice a year, and more frequently if needed. Firefighters can suggest that citizens change smoke alarm batteries in the spring and fall, coinciding with the adjustment of clocks for daylight saving time or standard time, to help them remember.

Flame Detectors

Flame detectors, also known as light detectors, and come in three basic types based on the spectrum of light they detect: ultraviolet (UV) detectors, infrared (IR) detectors, and detectors that can detect both types of light.

Flame detectors are highly sensitive in detecting fires, but they can also be triggered by non-fire conditions such as welding, sunlight, and other sources of bright light. To address this issue, flame detectors are typically positioned in areas where these light sources are unlikely, ensuring an unobstructed view of the protected area. If their line of sight is blocked by an opaque object, they will not activate.

Single-band IR detectors, which can be sensitive to sunlight, are often installed in fully enclosed areas to minimize false alarms. Most IR detectors are designed to require the presence of a flickering flame motion to initiate an alarm, further reducing false alarms.

On the other hand, ultraviolet detectors are virtually unaffected by sunlight, making them suitable for areas where IR detectors may not be feasible. However, they are not suitable for areas where welding activities take place or where intense mercury-vapor lamps are used.

Fire-Gas Detectors

Fire-gas detectors are designed to monitor and detect changes in the composition of the atmosphere within a confined space during a fire. The gases released by a fire can vary depending on the fuel involved, but commonly released gases include water vapor (H_2O), carbon dioxide (CO_2), carbon monoxide (CO), hydrogen chloride (HCl), hydrogen cyanide (HCN), hydrogen fluoride (HF), and hydrogen sulfide (H_2S).

For general fire detection purposes, it is practical to monitor the levels of carbon dioxide and carbon monoxide. These detectors can initiate an alarm signal faster than heat detectors but not as quickly as smoke detectors.

One significant advantage of fire-gas detectors is their ability to be more selective in detecting specific types of hostile fires while disregarding gases produced by friendly fires. This discrimination capability is important in distinguishing between different types of fires. Fire-gas detectors utilize semiconductors or catalytic elements to sense the presence of specific gases and transmit a signal to initiate the alarm.

Compared to other types of detectors, the use of fire-gas detectors is relatively limited, as they are specialized devices designed for specific applications. However, their ability to detect and discriminate between different fire gases makes them valuable in certain fire detection systems.

Combination Detectors

Combination detectors integrate multiple means of detection, such as heat and smoke detection, into a single device. These combination detectors offer increased versatility and responsiveness to different fire conditions. By combining different detection methods, they can provide enhanced fire detection capabilities.

Indicating Devices

In addition to detection devices, various audible and visible alarm-indicating devices are used. These devices serve to attract attention and alert occupants in the event of a fire. They can include loud sirens, electronic tones, bells, horns, chimes, or speakers broadcasting evacuation instructions. The choice of indicating device depends on the specific requirements of the environment and the needs of the occupants.

For environments with high noise levels or populations that require hearing protection, visual alarm indicators using high-intensity clear strobes may be used. These strobe indicators can be used alone or in combination with other audible alarm devices. They are particularly useful for meeting the requirements of the Americans with Disabilities Act (ADA) in areas where individuals with hearing impairments may be present.

Automatic Alarm Systems

Certain occupancies may be required by insurance carriers to have automatic alarm systems that transmit a signal to an off-site location to summon organized assistance in firefighting. These systems automatically initiate a response when the local alarm at the protected premises is activated. Different alarm systems employ various methods for signal transmission, including dedicated wire pairs, leased telephone lines, fiber-optic cables, or wireless communication links. The choice of communication method depends on the specific system and its requirements.

Building Evacuation

PEOPLE'S BEHAVIORS AND ACTIONS IN A FIRE

Certain characteristics and behaviors of occupants can influence their vulnerability and actions during a building fire. These factors include age, disabilities, panic behaviors, and firefighting behaviors.

Age and Vulnerability: Children under the age of five and the elderly over the age of sixty-five are at a higher risk of being victims in a building fire. The death rate from fire for these age groups is three times higher than the rest of the population. Although they represent only 20 percent of the population, they account for 45 percent of fire-related fatalities.

Panic Behavior: During a fire, some occupants may experience panic behavior, characterized by a sudden and excessive feeling of alarm or fear. In a state of panic, individuals may engage in irrational or extravagant efforts to secure their safety. Panic behavior can hinder effective evacuation and increase the risk of injury or becoming trapped.

Convergence Clusters: Convergence clusters occur when occupants in a burning building gather in specific rooms or areas that they perceive as safe havens. This behavior can lead to congestion and hinder the evacuation process, making it difficult for both the individuals seeking refuge and rescue personnel to navigate the space.

Reentry Behavior: After successfully evacuating a building, some individuals may reenter for various reasons. These reasons can include searching for loved ones, assisting others in exiting, or even attempting to help with firefighting efforts. While well-intentioned, reentry behavior can be extremely dangerous, as it exposes individuals to the risks associated with fire and hampers the work of emergency responders.

Occupant Firefighting Behavior: In some cases, individuals with economic or emotional ties to a building may engage in firefighting behavior. This behavior is predominantly seen in owners or occupants who have a strong attachment to the property and attempt to combat the fire using available resources. Engaging in firefighting without proper training and equipment can be hazardous and should be left to trained professionals.

PARTS OF AN EXIT

The means of egress in a building comprises three essential parts: exit access, exit, and exit discharge. These components ensure a safe path for occupants to evacuate during a fire or emergency situation.

1. Exit Access: The exit access refers to the designated route that individuals must take to reach the exit. It includes areas or pathways within the building that are specifically designed to be fire-protected, such as fire-rated hallways or corridors. These protected routes are crucial in providing a safe and clear path for occupants to reach the exit.

2. Exit: The exit itself is the final part of the egress system. It is the area where occupants can safely leave the building during an emergency. This can include doors, stairways, ramps, or other designated openings that lead to a place of safety, such as the exterior of the building or an enclosed exit stairwell. The exit should be clearly marked and easily accessible to allow for a swift and efficient evacuation.

3. Exit Discharge: The exit discharge is the area that separates the exit from the public or exterior space. It is the transition zone between the building's interior and the outside environment. Common examples of exit discharge include doorways or openings that lead from the building to the public sidewalk or open space outside the building. The exit discharge should be free from obstructions and provide a clear pathway for occupants to move away from the building and reach a safe location.

MEANS OF EGRESS REQUIREMENTS

Compliance with means of egress requirements is essential for ensuring the safety of building occupants during emergencies. Here are some key considerations and regulations related to means of egress:

1. Clear and Unobstructed Exits: Furnishings, decorations, or any other objects should not obstruct exits or access to them. It is crucial to maintain clear pathways to exits without any obstructions that could impede evacuation.

2. Door Requirements: Doors within the means of egress must meet applicable codes and standards. This includes factors such as door width, swing direction, construction materials, and the use of panic hardware. For rooms with a larger occupancy or those located in high-hazard areas, doors must swing in the direction of travel.

3. Stairs, Ramps, and Horizontal Exits: Stairs, ramps, and horizontal exits are important components of the means of egress. These elements should meet relevant standards regarding width, capacity, and number, ensuring they can accommodate the expected occupant load and allow for safe evacuation.

4. Minimum Width and Number of Exits: Applicable regulations specify the minimum width and number of exits required based on the occupancy and size of the building. Occupational Safety and Health Administration (OSHA), for instance, mandates that a minimum of two means of egress should be provided for every story or section, and they should be arranged in a way that minimizes the possibility of both being blocked by a single fire or emergency event.

5. Occupant Load: The occupant load determines the maximum number of individuals a means of egress is intended to serve. It is determined based on the occupancy type and use of the space. The means of egress must be designed to accommodate the expected occupant load and facilitate a safe evacuation.

6. Fire-Resistance and Separation: Means of egress components, such as doors and exits, may need to meet fire-resistance ratings and be separated by fire-resistant materials. These measures help prevent the spread of fire and maintain the integrity of the means of egress during an emergency.

7. Exit Discharge: The exit discharge is the area that leads directly outside or to a safe location. It should provide access to streets, walkways, refuge areas, public ways, or open spaces that lead to the outside. Exit doors within the means of egress must be unlocked and operable from the inside without the need for keys, tools, or specialized knowledge, ensuring easy egress for occupants.

Exit-Route Requirements

These are important requirements to ensure the safety and accessibility of exit routes in the workplace. Here is a summary of the exit-route requirements mentioned:

1. Ceiling Height: The ceiling of an exit route must be at least 7 feet 6 inches high to provide sufficient headroom for occupants.

2. Projection Limitations: Any projections from the ceiling, such as pipes or ducts, should not extend below 6 feet 8 inches from the floor to prevent obstruction and ensure clear passage.

3. Width Requirements: The width of the exit route should be adequate to accommodate the maximum permitted occupant load of each floor served by the exit route. The exit access should have a minimum width of 28 inches at all points.

4. Equal Width: If there is only one exit access leading to an exit or exit discharge, the width of the exit and exit discharge should be at least equal to the width of the exit access to maintain consistent egress capacity.

5. Obstruction Limitations: Objects or items that project into the exit route must not reduce the width of the route below the minimum width requirements.

6. Flammable and Explosive Hazards: Exit routes must be kept clear of explosive or highly flammable furnishings, decorations, or materials that could impede safe egress.

7. Unobstructed Paths: Exit routes must be free and unobstructed, ensuring that no materials or equipment are placed, either permanently or temporarily, within the exit route.

8. Lockable Rooms and Dead-Ends: The exit access should not go through a room that can be locked, such as a bathroom, and should not lead into a dead-end corridor that lacks a secondary means of egress.

9. Sloped Surfaces: If the exit route is not substantially level, stairs or ramps should be provided to facilitate safe and efficient egress.

10. Functioning Fire Protection Systems: Safeguards like sprinkler systems, alarm systems, fire doors, and exit lighting must be in proper working order at all times to enhance occupant safety during emergencies.

11. Exit Discharge: Exit discharges should lead occupants to a safe area outside the facility. If the discharge opens into a courtyard or open space, it should be large enough to accommodate all building occupants.

12. Maintenance during Construction or Repairs: Exit routes must be maintained during construction, repairs, or alterations to ensure they remain accessible and safe for occupants.

13. Occupancy during Repairs or Alterations: During repairs or alterations, employees should not occupy a workplace unless the required exit routes are available and existing fire protections are maintained or alternative fire protection is provided to ensure an equivalent level of safety.

14. Hazards during Construction or Repairs: Employees should not be exposed to hazards of flammable or explosive substances or equipment used during construction, repairs, or alterations that exceed normal permissible conditions, as it may impede their ability to safely exit the workplace.

These requirements help ensure that exit routes are properly designed, maintained, and accessible, allowing for the safe evacuation of occupants during emergencies in the workplace. It is important for employers to comply with these regulations to prioritize the safety of their employees.

Illumination and Emergency Lighting

Proper illumination and emergency lighting are crucial for the safe evacuation of occupants during an emergency. Here are the key points regarding lighting requirements in exit routes:

1. Adequate Illumination: Lighting and markings must be sufficient and appropriate to ensure that employees with normal vision can see along the exit route clearly. This ensures that occupants can navigate the path of egress without any hindrances.

2. Natural Lighting: In structures that are occupied only during daylight hours, the life-safety codes require the means of egress to be illuminated with natural lighting. The natural lighting should provide the required level of illumination to facilitate safe evacuation.

3. Emergency Lighting: In addition to normal lighting, emergency lighting is necessary to maintain illumination during power failures or other emergencies. Emergency lighting should be provided throughout the means of egress.

4. Illumination Level and Duration: Emergency lighting should have a sufficient illumination level to ensure visibility and last for at least one and a half hours in the event of a failure of normal lighting. This duration allows occupants to safely evacuate even if the power supply is disrupted.

5. Illumination Standards: The illumination levels for emergency lighting should not be less than an average of 1 foot-candle, which is a unit of light intensity. Additionally, at any point along the path of egress at floor level, the illumination should not be less than 0.1 foot-candle. These standards ensure that the exit route remains adequately lit for safe evacuation.

By ensuring proper illumination and emergency lighting, employers can enhance the visibility and safety of occupants during an emergency, enabling them to locate and follow the designated exit routes effectively. Regular maintenance and testing of emergency lighting systems are essential to ensure their reliable operation when needed.

Exit Signs

Exit signage plays a critical role in guiding occupants towards safe egress routes during emergencies. Here are the key points regarding exit signs and markings:

1. Marking Exits: Life-safety codes require that exits, excluding main exterior exit doors that are clearly identifiable as exits, must be marked with an approved sign. These signs should be readily visible from any direction of exit access.

2. Illumination: Exit signs must be illuminated to a surface value of at least five foot-candles. Adequate illumination ensures that the signs remain visible even in low-light conditions. Self-luminous or electroluminescent signs with a minimum luminance value of 0.06 foot-lamberts are also permitted.

3. Distinctive Color: Exit signs should be distinctive in color, making them easily distinguishable from their surroundings. The specific color requirements may vary depending on the applicable codes or standards.

4. Legibility: Each exit sign must prominently display the word "EXIT" in plainly legible letters that are at least 6 inches high. The principal strokes of the letters in the word "EXIT" should be at least three-fourths of an inch wide. Clear and visible lettering ensures that occupants can quickly identify the exit signs.

5. Clear Visibility: Exit-route doors should be free of decorations or signs that obstruct their visibility. It is crucial to maintain a clear line of sight to exit signs at all times to aid in swift evacuation.

6. Directional Signage: If the direction of travel to the exit or exit discharge is not immediately apparent, signs must be posted along the exit access to indicate the direction of the nearest exit and exit discharge. These signs help occupants navigate through the exit route effectively.

7. Marking Non-Exits: Doorways or passages along the exit access that could be mistaken for an exit must be marked with signs indicating that they are not an exit. Common designations include "Not an Exit" or signs indicating the actual use of the space, such as "Closet."

By properly marking exits and using clear and visible signage, occupants can easily locate and follow the designated egress routes, ensuring a safe and efficient evacuation during emergencies. Regular inspections and maintenance of exit signs and markings are important to ensure their visibility and legibility over time.

Sprinkler Systems

Certain occupancies are mandated by life-safety codes to have sprinkler systems installed. New high-rise industrial occupancies typically require automatic sprinklers, although general, low-hazard, or special-purpose industrial occupancies may be exempted from this requirement.

Building Contents

Building contents play a crucial role in the fire loading of a building and significantly impact the spread of smoke and flames, making them a vital consideration for life safety. Contents encompass objects, goods, or products that are placed within a structure for functional, operational, or decorative purposes, excluding the building's structural elements, service equipment, and items classified as interior finish. These contents serve as fuel for fires. When evaluating building contents, it is important to consider the likelihood of combustible materials igniting, the potential for flames and heat to spread, the generation of smoke and gases, and the risk of explosions or structural failure that could endanger occupants. Additionally, the interior finish of the building, including exposed surfaces of walls, ceilings, and floors, is subject to flame spread limitations and specific material requirements in areas such as exits, access routes, and other designated areas of the building as outlined in life-safety codes.

Interior Finishes

In industrial occupancies, the interior finishes must adhere to the life-safety requirements outlined by the respective National Fire Protection Agency of a country. These requirements pertain to the materials used for interior walls and ceilings in terms of their flame spread and smoke development characteristics. The NFPA of

U.S.A categorizes interior finishes into three classes: Class A, Class B, and Class C, based on their performance in flame spread and smoke development tests. The criteria for each class are as follows:

- Class A Interior Wall and Ceiling Finish: This class has the most stringent requirements, with a flame spread rating of 0-25 and a smoke development rating of 0-450. These materials exhibit excellent fire resistance and produce minimal smoke during a fire event.

- Class B Interior Wall and Ceiling Finish: Materials in this class have a flame spread rating of 26-75 and a smoke development rating of 0-450. While they have a moderate level of fire resistance, they still provide a reasonable degree of safety by limiting the spread of flames and smoke.

- Class C Interior Wall and Ceiling Finish: This class includes materials with a flame spread rating of 76-200 and a smoke development rating of 0-450. Class C finishes offer a lower level of fire resistance compared to Class A and Class B materials, but they still contribute to controlling flame spread and smoke development.

In addition to interior wall and ceiling finishes, it is also important to consider the selection of floor finishes such as wood, carpet, tile, and others. Floor finishes should be chosen with fire safety in mind, taking into account factors like flame spread, smoke generation, and ease of evacuation in the event of a fire.

Detection, Alarm, and Communications Systems

Detection, alarm, and communications systems play a crucial role in identifying fires early, alerting building occupants to the potential danger, and notifying the fire department for prompt response. In industrial occupancies, regulatory authorities mandates the installation of a fire alarm system, except in cases where the total building capacity is below one hundred individuals, with fewer than twenty-five located above or below the exit discharge level.

There are several means by which an alarm can be initiated, such as:

1. Manual Means: Activation of the fire alarm system can be done manually by individuals upon discovering a fire or by operating a manual fire alarm box located within the premises.

2. Approved Automatic Fire-Detection System with Manual Fire Alarm Box: An automatic fire-detection system that meets approved standards can serve as a means of alarm initiation. Additionally, at least one manual fire alarm box must be present for manual activation if needed.

3. Approved, Supervised Automatic Sprinkler System with Manual Fire Alarm Box: In cases where an approved, supervised automatic sprinkler system is installed, it can serve as an alarm initiation method. Alongside this, a minimum of one manual fire alarm box should be available for manual activation if required.

These requirements ensure that there are reliable means to detect and signal the presence of a fire, allowing for timely evacuation and appropriate actions to be taken.

Occupant Notification

In addition to the fire alarm system, laws mandates that employers install and maintain an operable employee alarm system that provides a distinct signal to alert employees of a fire or other emergencies. This requirement applies unless employees are able to

promptly detect a fire or other hazards through visual or olfactory cues, allowing them to be adequately warned.

In high-hazard industrial occupancies, the fire alarm system should be designed to automatically initiate an occupant-evacuation alarm signal. This ensures that in case of a fire, the alarm system will promptly and automatically trigger an alarm specifically intended to notify occupants to evacuate the building swiftly and safely.

These measures help to ensure that employees are promptly alerted to the presence of a fire or other emergencies, enabling them to take immediate action to protect their safety and evacuate the premises in a timely manner.

Building Services

Building services play a crucial role in ensuring the safety of occupants during fire or other emergency situations. Life-safety codes establish specific requirements for various building utilities and services, including heating, ventilation, and air-conditioning equipment. These codes address ventilation aspects, such as mechanical ventilation systems and pressurized stair-enclosure systems, to control the movement of smoke and maintain safe conditions during evacuations. Additionally, life-safety codes outline the necessary protection measures for components such as rubbish chutes, incinerators, laundry chutes, elevators, escalators, and conveyors to prevent the spread of fire within the building.

Employee Emergency Action Plan

To ensure the safe evacuation of all individuals during a fire or emergency, employers must develop an employee emergency action plan. This plan should incorporate the following components:

1. Reporting Procedures: Clear instructions on how to report a fire or emergency should be provided to employees.

2. Evacuation Procedures: The plan must outline procedures for emergency evacuation, including the type of evacuation and assignments for exit routes.

3. Critical Plant Operations: Procedures should be established to determine which employees will remain to operate critical plant operations before evacuating.

4. Employee Accountability: The plan should include procedures for accounting for all employees after evacuation to ensure everyone's safety.

5. Rescue and Medical Duties: Procedures should be outlined for employees who are assigned to perform rescue or medical duties during emergencies.

6. Points of Contact: The plan should identify the names or job titles of employees who can provide additional information or clarify duties under the plan.

In addition to the emergency action plan, employers must have effective means of notifying building occupants in the event of a fire. The notification signal should be distinctive, enabling workers to differentiate it from other alarms and understand its significance. Employee training is a crucial aspect of the emergency action plan. Employers should designate and train specific employees to assist in the safe and orderly evacuation of their coworkers. Employers to review the emergency action plan with each employee at the following times:

- During plan development or when an employee is initially assigned to a job

- When there are changes to the employee's responsibilities under the plan

- Whenever modifications are made to the plan

By adhering to these guidelines, employers can enhance the effectiveness of their emergency preparedness efforts and ensure the well-being of their employees during critical situations.

Fire Program Management

INTRODUCTION

In today's competitive business landscape, companies recognize the importance of minimizing losses from fire or emergency incidents. Developing and implementing effective fire-risk management programs has proven to be a crucial factor in achieving this goal. These programs aim to identify, evaluate, and control hazards, ensuring the protection of employees, the public, the environment, and company assets. The process involves the following key steps:

1. Identification of Hazards: The first step involves identifying potential fire and emergency hazards or events that could lead to significant losses.

2. Risk Quantification: The next step is to quantify the risk associated with these hazards, considering the probability of occurrence and the potential consequences of fire or emergency events.

3. Prevention and Protection Strategies: Once the risks are understood, alternative prevention and protection strategies are developed and evaluated. These strategies aim to reduce the fire and emergency risk effectively.

4. Measurement of Effectiveness: The implemented prevention and protection strategies are measured to determine their effectiveness in reducing the fire and emergency risks. Regular evaluation helps assess the impact of these strategies and make any necessary adjustments.

Conducting a comprehensive risk assessment using these four steps provides decision-makers with valuable insights into the potential risks present in their facilities and the ability to withstand fire or emergency incidents. It's important to note that the specific responsibilities of a safety professional in this process may vary depending on the organizational structure and culture.

By following these steps, safety professionals can fulfill their common responsibilities and contribute to the development and implementation of robust fire-risk management programs within their organizations.

HAZARD IDENTIFICATION

Hazard identification is a critical process that involves recognizing potential hazards that can lead to significant losses. It should begin during the preplanning stages, evaluating new materials, processes, and production modifications, and continue through inspections of existing facilities. The safety professional plays a key role in providing technical knowledge related to fire codes and standards that can be used to identify actual or potential fire hazards. These codes may include from regulatory authorities like for example NFPA codes, HSE regulations, local building codes, OSHA standards, and relevant insurance standards like those from Factory Mutual.

To effectively identify hazards, the safety professional should have a deep understanding of these standards and codes and how they apply to specific situations. For instance, in the case of new construction, the safety professional may evaluate the site for various factors, such as:

- Exposure to natural disasters like floods or adjacent facility and process hazards.

- Availability of sufficient water supply for fire protection.

- Suitability of local emergency support forces, such as the fire department.

- Presence of access impediments like traffic, terrain, or nearby buildings.

- Incorporation of building design elements such as fire-resistant materials, fire area segregation for high-value or high-hazard areas, alarm and automatic suppression systems, and adequate exits.

Reference materials like NFPA's Industrial Fire Hazards Handbook, various NFPA codes, and insurance publications can be utilized to describe fire hazards in different industries and special-process hazards based on current technology and past incidents.

By effectively identifying hazards and considering relevant standards and codes, safety professionals can contribute to creating safer environments and minimizing the risk of fire-related incidents.

QUANTIFICATION OF RISK

After identifying a fire hazard, the next step is to assess the risk associated with it. The extent and method of risk assessment depend on factors such as cost, time limitations, the significance of the decision, and the complexity of the problem. Simple code-compliance issues may require straightforward choices, while more complex problems involving new technologies or high-hazard operations necessitate more detailed risk assessment methods.

A fundamental risk assessment involves evaluating the probability and severity of potential fire losses. It's important to acknowledge the element of uncertainty associated with both factors. Two approaches for determining the probability values for fire events are objective and subjective estimation. Objective estimation utilizes available data on loss-event frequencies to develop probability values, which must be reliable and valid. Subjective estimation, on the other hand, employs inferential judgment based on loss-trending information, such as equipment failures, human error, ignition sources, loss-control elements, and damageability factors. The NFPA Fire Analysis and Research Division is a valuable source for such information. In recent years, formalized risk assessment methods that integrate statistical data, deterministic models, and expert opinion have gained popularity in supporting decisions on fire-safety issues.

When evaluating the severity of a fire risk, both direct and indirect loss potentials should be considered. Direct losses encompass business interruption, liability for injury or death, environmental contamination, and damage to the company's image. Most quantification studies express loss potential in equivalent monetary terms.

Once the probability and severity of the fire risk are determined, this data is used to assess the acceptability of the risk. If the risk is deemed acceptable, immediate action may not be necessary, but ongoing monitoring is still required to detect any changes that could render the risk unacceptable. If the risk is deemed unacceptable, decisions must be made on how to address it. Some general options for handling fire-risk exposure include:

1. Avoiding the risk by refraining from engaging in the activity.

2. Transferring the risk by obtaining insurance coverage or making alternative risk-transfer arrangements, such as self-insurance.

3. Implementing loss-control improvements.

4. Developing a risk-management program that combines the above options.

The latter two options are common responsibilities of safety professionals and are integral to the third step in the risk-assessment process: the development of fire-protection and prevention strategies.

FIRE PROTECTION AND PREVENTION STRATEGIES

Safety professionals play a crucial role in recommending appropriate fire prevention and protection strategies for organizations. These strategies can be broadly categorized into engineering controls and administrative controls. Engineering controls are prioritized as they have the potential to eliminate fire or explosion risks. Examples of engineering controls include substituting flammable liquids with nonflammable ones, implementing pressure-relief devices, using explosion-proof electrical wiring, and ensuring proper ventilation in spray-painting booths. These controls aim to eliminate ignition sources, prevent excessive pressure buildup, or reduce the concentration of flammable gases or vapors below their flammable limits. It should be noted that some engineering controls do not eliminate the risk entirely but rather minimize the damage once a fire starts, such as automatic sprinkler systems. Safety professionals are also responsible for coordinating the inspection, testing, and maintenance of fire suppression systems once they are installed.

The fourth option for risk control involves the development, implementation, and monitoring of fire risk management programs. Safety professionals are actively involved in the development of these programs, which should be documented and clearly define their purpose and scope.

Employee training is an integral part of many fire risk management programs. This training may include instruction on the use of fire extinguishers, emergency response procedures, and participation in a fire brigade if one exists in the establishment. The U.S. Fire Administration, a part of the Federal Emergency Management Agency (FEMA), is an excellent resource for fire safety training.

Another responsibility of safety professionals in fire program management is the development and evaluation of fire response strategies. In the wake of significant events like the September 11, 2001 attacks, these responsibilities have expanded beyond simple fire response plans to encompass emergency response plans.

When making risk management decisions that involve implementing loss control improvements, it may be necessary to conduct a cost-benefit analysis. Determining the cost of fire loss control alternatives, including design, installation, system maintenance, and training expenses, is usually straightforward. However, evaluating the benefits or the extent of risk reduction is more challenging. It requires assessing the reduced probability of fire occurrence and the potential decrease in severity, which involves exercising considerable judgment. Insurance reports and the National Fire Incident Reporting System can provide valuable information about loss experience. Fire protection engineering analysis can assist in estimating fire risk after implementing control strategies. Additionally, safety professionals can utilize computer modeling, which integrates deterministic fire hazard modeling, probabilistic modeling, and risk profile information, to aid in risk assessment.

MEASUREMENT OF THE EFFECTIVENESS OF FIRE STRATEGIES

The final step in the fire program management process involves measuring the effectiveness of the implemented fire strategies. This step includes reevaluating the probability of fire risk after the strategies have been successfully implemented. The goal is to achieve the level of risk reduction identified during the cost-benefit analysis conducted earlier. Measuring effectiveness is crucial for all strategies, but it holds particular importance for fire risk management programs.

It is important to emphasize that the written program itself is only effective if it is properly implemented. Therefore, the safety professional plays a critical role in measuring and evaluating the program's implementation to ensure its effectiveness in reducing fire risk.

In summary, a well-executed risk assessment provides management with insights into the relative level of risk a facility may face, the facility's level of preparedness to handle a fire or emergency, and its ability to survive and continue operating during an emergency situation.

EMERGENCY RESPONSE PLANS

An emergency response plan is a crucial standard operating procedure for addressing various types of emergencies. While traditional plans focused on fire and natural disasters, today's risks have evolved significantly, encompassing cyber-terrorism, product tampering, biological attacks, and ecological terrorism. These emerging threats require proactive measures and comprehensive planning to minimize risks and mitigate damages.

The development of an emergency-response plan is a vital responsibility of the safety professional, ensuring coordinated reactions to minimize and prevent further damage to assets. To assist in fulfilling this responsibility, the following key points are discussed:

- Overview of Federal regulations and recommendations pertaining to emergency response plans.
- Preplanning activities necessary for developing an effective response plan.
- Suggestions for elements to include in a comprehensive response plan.

Federal agencies, including the Federal Emergency Management Agency (FEMA), the Occupational Safety and Health Administration (OSHA), the Environmental Protection Agency (EPA), the Health & Safety Executive HSE (UK), mandate emergency response plans based on specific requirements. NFPA 1600 also provides recommended practices for emergency management planning in both public and private organizations. Core planning areas recommended by NFPA 1600 include hazard assessment and mitigation, preparedness, response, recovery, and training/evaluation.

In summary, a concise and well-developed emergency response plan is essential for effective preparedness, coordination, and response to a wide range of emergencies, safeguarding the organization and minimizing potential damages.

PLANNING AN EMERGENCY-RESPONSE STRATEGY

Planning an effective emergency-response strategy begins with facility management taking responsibility for implementing and regularly evaluating an emergency-response program. To ensure effectiveness, input and support from all employees and the community are necessary. This involves establishing an emergency-response committee responsible for coordinating the plan's development, implementation, training, drills, equipment, and evaluation. The committee should include representatives from various departments within the facility, community emergency-response agencies, and management, maintenance, engineering, transportation, safety, and human resources personnel. Maintaining ongoing relationships and communication with community emergency-response agencies is crucial.

The initial task of the emergency-response committee is to identify potential risks, assess their viability, evaluate the probability of occurrence, and estimate potential damages. This survey focuses on facility operations, processes, raw materials, as well as prevention and preparedness measures. It includes assessing natural risks (e.g., earthquakes, hurricanes) and man-made risks (e.g., fires, hazardous-material incidents, workplace violence). The committee should also review facility information such as drawings, process-flow diagrams, contact lists, material-safety datasheets, evacuation plans, training records, and community emergency plans.

Each facility must be individually assessed to identify actual or potential emergency risks, and a customized emergency-response program should be developed and implemented accordingly. The committee must also determine the organization's commitment of time and resources to developing and implementing the plan, considering costs such as personal protective equipment, emergency equipment and supplies, medical expenses, and training. Conducting drills regularly for all employees and community emergency-response agencies is essential but can be costly and time-consuming.

Evaluating the support and capabilities of local community emergency-response agencies is crucial, considering factors like their organization type (paid or volunteer), available equipment, response times, and member training. Planning may also involve establishing formal agreements with nearby organizations to provide assistance during emergencies. Communication with the community, employees, emergency-response agencies, regulatory bodies, and the media should be carefully considered, ensuring accurate and effective dissemination of information.

Pre-incident planning by the emergency-response committee benefits all parties involved, leading to safer response activities and minimized property loss. It is an ongoing process that requires commitment, communication, and cooperation among all organizations involved in emergency response. Facility changes should be continuously evaluated for their impact on emergency risks and responses.

In summary, effective emergency-response planning involves forming a dedicated committee, assessing risks, developing a customized response program, allocating resources, evaluating community support, establishing partnerships, and ensuring clear communication channels. Continual assessment and adaptation are necessary to keep up with facility changes and ensure preparedness.

DEVELOPING THE WRITTEN EMERGENCY – RESPONSE PLAN

After completing the risk assessment and reviewing relevant regulations, the emergency-response committee is now prepared to develop a written draft of the emergency-response plan. While there are various model plans available, it is recommended to use the Integrated Contingency Plan (ICP) as a benchmark.

The ICP was collaboratively developed by the Research and Special Programs Administration and OSHA. It aims to guide facility management in creating a single, comprehensive emergency-response plan that replaces the need for multiple plans to comply with different regulations.

The structure of the ICP is based on the National Interagency Incident Management System (NIIMS) Incident Command System (ICS), which is widely recognized and used by federal, state, and local organizations. The ICP format consists of three main sections: an introduction, a core plan, and supporting annexes.

The core plan outlines the essential steps required to initiate, conduct, and conclude an emergency-response action, including recognition, notification, and initial response. It incorporates a hierarchical approach to match the emergency's nature and potential impacts with appropriate resources, personnel, and response actions. The development of response levels should align with efforts taken by the Local Emergency Planning Committee (LEPC) or mutual aid organizations. Checklists or flowcharts based on response levels can serve as the foundation for the core plan.

The annexes in the ICP provide supporting information for executing the emergency response outlined in the core plan. They also address regulatory requirements not covered elsewhere in the ICP. Annexes 1 to 3 offer detailed information specific to encountered hazards, encouraging the use of concise checklists or flowcharts. Annexes 4 to 8 include non-critical information such as cross-references for regulatory compliance and background planning details.

In conclusion, an emergency-response plan serves as the foundation for operations during an emergency, providing vital information for the incident commander to implement appropriate strategies and tactics. While the use of the ICP model is not federally mandated, it is the preferred method of response planning. Implementing the ICP model reduces duplication of plans within a facility, improves efficiency for both regulated and regulating communities, and minimizes confusion among facility first responders who must determine the applicable plan. By adopting a single integrated plan, coordination between facility and external response personnel is enhanced. This approach also reduces costs associated with preparing, maintaining, submitting, and updating multiple plans.

EMERGENCY MEDICAL CARE

Emergency response plans should include provisions for emergency medical care, as injuries and illnesses requiring immediate medical attention are likely to occur during most emergencies. Minimizing the impact of such incidents heavily relies on response time. Therefore, emergency response planning should begin with a survey of local medical facilities to assess their capabilities and response times. Arrangements can then be made based on these facilities' capabilities, and ambulance services should be familiar with the facility's location and access routes in advance.

- The employer must ensure the availability of medical personnel for advice and consultation on matters of plant health.
- Suitable facilities for quick drenching or flushing of the eyes and body must be provided within the work area for immediate emergency use if there is a risk of exposure to corrosive materials.
- If there is no nearby infirmary, clinic, or hospital used for treating injured employees, at least one person must be adequately trained to render first aid. Adequate first aid supplies should also be readily available.

Two key terms in this standard require clarification:

- Near proximity: In areas where accidents resulting in life-threatening or permanently disabling injuries or illnesses can be expected, a three- to four-minute response time, from the time of injury to the administration of first aid, is required. In other situations where life-threatening or permanently disabling injuries are less likely, a longer response time, such as fifteen minutes, is considered acceptable.

- Adequate training: various topics for first aid training, including teaching methods, responding to health emergencies, surveying the scene, basic adult cardiopulmonary resuscitation (CPR), basic first aid intervention, universal precautions, first aid supplies, trainee assessments, and program updates. Refresher training for CPR should be conducted annually, while first aid training should be refreshed every three years.

Exact requirements for first aid supplies cannot be provided since they vary depending on the workplace. Each workplace should be evaluated on a case-by-case basis, considering the types of injuries and illnesses likely to occur. Safety professionals may consult with the local fire and rescue department or a licensed healthcare provider to assist in evaluating the appropriate supplies.

Additionally, preplacement medical examinations and medical surveillance are crucial aspects of medical services for emergency response teams. Before assigning personnel to these teams, employers must ensure that employees are physically capable of performing the assigned duties.

TRAINING

Training is of utmost importance for the successful implementation of an emergency plan. When discussing training, distinguish between two terms: education and training. Education refers to the process of imparting knowledge or skill through systematic instruction, while training involves making trainees proficient through instruction and practical experience in operating equipment required for their assigned duties. Prior to implementing an emergency action plan, an adequate number of individuals must receive training to effectively administer critical elements of the plan. All other employees should be trained on how to respond to various types of emergencies. Additionally, specialized training is necessary for key personnel, while other employees should be trained in the following areas:

1. Emergency escape procedures, including exit routes and alarm recognition.

2. Procedures for employees who need to remain behind to operate critical plant operations or shut down equipment before evacuating.

3. Procedures for accounting for all employees after completing emergency evacuations.

4. Rescue and medical duties for employees assigned to perform them.

5. Preferred methods of reporting emergencies.

Initial emergency response training should be conducted when the plan is developed and for all new employees. Refresher and supplemental training should occur annually, as well as when new equipment, materials, or processes are introduced, procedures are updated or revised, or drills or actual emergencies reveal areas for improvement that need to be communicated to employees. Following training, employers should certify that workers have received and successfully completed the specified training.

Emergency drills play a vital role in emergency response and serve as an evaluation tool for assessing the effectiveness of planning. These drills should ideally be conducted at random intervals and at least once a year. A well-designed drill allows all participants, including external response agencies, to practice their trained responses. Documenting drill details such as the timing of alarm activations and the evaluation of employees and response agencies helps assess the effectiveness of both the emergency plan and the training. In buildings or industrial parks where multiple employers are present, emergency plans should be coordinated with other companies and employees in the same building or industrial park.

PERSONAL PROTECTIVE EQUIPMENT

Personal protective equipment (PPE) is a crucial consideration in fire program management, particularly in the realm of emergency response planning. It is vital to ensure effective personal protection for individuals who may be exposed to potentially hazardous substances during emergency incidents. Various hazardous circumstances can arise during emergencies, including:

- Fire, smoke, and electricity hazards.
- Chemical splashes or contact with toxic materials.
- Explosion hazards, such as flying particles.
- Unknown atmospheres that may have insufficient oxygen levels or contain toxic gases, vapors, and mists.

In such situations, it is of utmost importance to provide employees with adequate protection. Additionally, these employees must undergo medical clearance to ensure their ability to wear PPE safely.

MEDIA CONTROL

In accordance with the ICP model emergency-response plan, it is crucial to incorporate effective communication strategies with the media during emergencies. To ensure the organization presents accurate information and manages public perception, it is important to address all potential channels of information flow. Here are some suggested measures for addressing the media as part of the overall emergency-response plan:

- Designate a safe area away from emergency traffic for media vehicles and communications.
- Maintain security in the designated media area, preventing media representatives from accessing the emergency site.
- Appoint a specific member of management as the spokesperson for the company, restricting other employees from engaging with the media. The selected individual should possess experience in public relations and media interactions.
- Direct the media to appropriate areas for capturing video footage, as needed.
- Provide informational packets containing company details to the media.
- Prior to presenting information to the media, ensure it is reviewed by legal counsel, and limit the number of questions from the media.

If the emergency involves environmental spills, the EPA's Community Relations Program can be a valuable resource. This program aims to achieve three primary objectives:

- Inform the community about the health and environmental impacts of the release and the response actions being considered.
- Encourage citizens to provide information about the site and its surroundings and express any concerns regarding the actions being undertaken.
- Incorporate citizen comments and concerns into the decision-making process at the emergency-response site.

An official spokesperson from the EPA is appointed for each emergency-response action to keep the public informed and address any questions. Engaging with the community, responding to media inquiries, and providing local officials with site-status information are among the activities that the EPA is likely to undertake.

RECOVERY AFTER AN EMERGENCY

An effective emergency-response plan must include a well-developed business recovery plan to ensure the organization's continuity after an incident. Business recovery begins immediately after the emergency phase of the incident is over. Over the past fifteen years, the focus of business recovery has expanded to encompass the recovery of the entire business, including technology, personnel, and processes. The goal is to ensure that the organization can continue its operations after an incident. Failure to have a formal business recovery plan significantly increases the risk of not recovering and potentially going out of business. An emergency incident can lead to various detrimental consequences, such as lost production, delayed invoicing and wage payments, unpaid suppliers, missed or lost orders, and a loss of customer confidence.

There are numerous books and computer software programs available that provide valuable guidance for developing a business recovery plan. These resources can be helpful in the planning process. Generally, there are four essential steps in developing a recovery plan.

The first step is to identify an individual or a team responsible for the development and implementation of the business recovery plan. This person or team will collaborate with relevant agencies and organizations involved in business recovery activities.

The second step is to conduct a business impact assessment to determine the operational and financial consequences of business processes becoming inoperable. This assessment serves as the foundation for formulating the organization's business recovery strategy, which aims to restore operations within the required time frames. Information about the incident's effect and its impact on downtime is gathered through interviews with management. This information is analyzed to develop business, operational impact, and financial impact analyses for each function.

The business analysis identifies and describes critical business functions and the high-level resources that support them. It also considers the customers served by these functions. This analysis helps determine the relative importance of different business processes and assists management in identifying measures to avoid downtime.

The operational impact analysis focuses on the organizational implications associated with the loss of facility access or use, including the complete loss of a facility. It identifies which functions may be interrupted by an incident and the consequences for customers resulting from such interruptions.

The financial impact analysis identifies the economic losses that could result from an incident and the resulting downtime of a business unit. The outcomes of this analysis can provide cost justification for implementing and maintaining specific recovery strategies.

The third step involves developing a business recovery strategy that defines the specific resources necessary for the performance of each critical business unit function. It also outlines recommended strategies for recovering those resources in the event of downtime. This strategy provides detailed guidelines for plan implementation. These guidelines are developed in consultation with business unit managers, who identify the specific resources required for full and partial operation of various business units. The identified resources are then organized into logical categories based on their recovery needs.

It is important for the guidelines to describe recovery alternatives for each category identified above. This allows for the selection of the most effective approach from each set of alternatives, considering the organization's continuity and budget requirements.

The fourth and final step is the implementation and evaluation of the business recovery plan. This includes documenting the procedures and plans for each business unit, as well as administering the overall plan, which encompasses high-level contingency management procedures.

Many organizations' recovery strategies rely on internal and external contracts and arrangements as tools for recovery. Therefore, the plan should document any necessary instructions to utilize these contracts effectively. Business unit managers should be actively involved in this phase to ensure their ownership of the program once the implementation is complete.

INVESTIGATION OF EMERGENCY INCIDENTS

Investigating incidents that result in or have the potential to cause major releases, fires, or explosions is crucial for preventing future losses. The primary objective of these investigations is to determine the causes of the incidents so that appropriate preventive measures can be implemented.

As a general practice, incident investigations should be initiated promptly after the emergency phase of the incident. Investigators should possess knowledge of the plant and process, as well as training in loss incident investigation. It is important for the organization to develop a formal written form for loss incident investigations, which should include essential information such as the date of the incident, date of investigation, names of investigators, incident description, causal factors, and resulting recommendations. These incident reports should be reviewed by relevant personnel within the facility.

Fire investigations have four main objectives: reviewing structural damage, examining the fire ignition sequence, analyzing fire development, and assessing fire casualties. The investigation typically starts with an examination of the exterior of the structure to document any fire or firefighting-related damage. The interior of the structure is then reviewed to document fire damage or other impacts caused by firefighting efforts.

After completing the review of the exterior and interior, the investigator aims to reconstruct the fire. This involves identifying the fire's origin, the location of combustible materials, and the sequence of events that led to ignition. The investigation considers the heat source, the combustible materials involved, and the actions that brought them into contact. The contents of the building, including ordinary combustibles, are evaluated for their influence on fire growth and the production of smoke and gases. Structural features such as compartmentation, fire walls, interior finish, and concealed spaces are also investigated to understand their impact on fire development.

Following the reconstruction of the fire, the investigator conducts interviews with witnesses and firefighters present at the scene. These interviews provide valuable observations about various conditions, such as flame spread, heat generated, smoke volume and color, property damage, security issues, and any unusual activities. In some cases, laboratory tests may be necessary to evaluate the burn characteristics of materials, analyze residues, or examine potential failures in mechanical equipment like heaters. If equipment failure is suspected, service and maintenance records of the equipment may need to be reviewed.

Once all the relevant information is gathered, the investigator analyzes it to determine the causes of the incident. This analysis focuses on both surface causes, which are related to unsafe acts or conditions, and underlying causes, which stem from deficiencies in management systems that allowed those unsafe acts or conditions to exist. It is crucial to identify all causes and develop appropriate recommendations to prevent future incidents. Additionally, accurate information and documentation from investigations are essential for insurance and legal purposes. Recommendations should prioritize engineering controls, followed by administrative controls. Effective investigations include follow-up to ensure the recommendations have been successful in reducing or eliminating the fire causes. It is important to note that fire casualties or suspected arson cases are typically investigated by local fire marshals or police departments.

The remaining section will cover other important responsibilities of safety professionals in fire program management, such as maintaining fire protection systems, conducting fire inspections, and managing hot work permit programs.

MAINTENANCE OF FIRE-PROTECTION SYSTEMS

Fire-protection systems play a crucial role in mitigating fire losses in industrial facilities. Unfortunately, instances of significant fire losses due to malfunctioning fire-protection equipment still occur due to various reasons, such as closed sprinkler water-control valves, inoperative fire pumps, faulty fire detectors, alarm systems, and sprinkler heads. While maintenance requirements for fire-protection systems have been addressed earlier, this chapter focuses on developing procedures to follow when any fire system becomes inoperable due to maintenance, renovation, equipment failure, or an emergency incident.

Having effective procedures during fire-system shutdown is vital in minimizing the risk of fire losses. These procedures should be documented and include the following:

- Designate an individual, such as a maintenance supervisor or a plant engineer, with the responsibility and authority to control the shutdown of fire systems. Immediate notification of any fire-safety system shutdowns should be provided to this individual.
- Provide training and education for all personnel involved in the shutdown procedures.
- Limit the affected area during the shutdown.
- Complement manual fire protection measures, such as portable fire extinguishers, with automatic fire suppression systems in the shutdown area.
- Avoid hot work and other operations that generate sparks within the shutdown area.
- Verify the operational status of fire-protection systems through testing.
- Shut down or isolate any hazardous production operations in the area where the fire-protection system is being shut down.
- Apply "lockout" or "tagout" procedures to impaired fire-protection systems.
- Notify the public fire department, central station, or alarm company about the fire system shutdown and provide details on the extent of the system's outage.
- Complete the necessary work promptly to minimize the duration of the shutdown.
- Restore any disconnected fire-protection equipment, alarms, or detection devices.
- Verify the operational status of fire-protection systems through testing, ensure portable extinguishers are in place and fully charged, and confirm the return of hose lines.
- Notify plant personnel and the public fire department, central station, or alarm company once the fire-protection systems have been restored.

FIRE INSPECTIONS

Implementing an inspection program for fire safety is just as important as maintaining fire-protection systems in a plant. These inspections can be conducted as part of a broader safety inspection or specifically focused on fire hazards and fire-protection systems. It is crucial to have knowledgeable individuals who are trained in equipment operation and testing to conduct these inspections once an adequate program has been established and implemented. Monthly inspections should be carried out as a minimum requirement.

To streamline facility safety inspections, it is recommended to use written forms tailored to the specific occupancy and equipment. These forms should be comprehensive to ensure no aspect of prevention or protection is overlooked. The inspections must identify all deficiencies, provide suitable recommendations, and assign responsibilities for correction and follow-up actions. Some areas to address in a fire safety inspection include:

- Potential fuel sources, such as poor housekeeping, improper storage of ordinary combustibles, and incorrect usage and storage of flammable or combustible liquids.
- Potential ignition sources, such as smoking, electrical deficiencies, static charges, and heating appliances.
- Life-safety issues, including blocked exits, aisle ways, exit signs, and fire doors.
- Compliance with procedures like hot work procedures, fire system shutdowns, fire system maintenance, emergency evacuation systems, and portable fire extinguishers.

Once the inspections are completed, the written forms or reports should be forwarded to facility management for review and necessary actions. Any severe deficiencies posing imminent danger should be immediately reported to facility management to initiate corrective measures. Fire-safety inspections play a critical role in the overall safety program as they proactively identify and address fire hazards before they lead to loss incidents.

HOT-WORK PERMIT PROGRAMS

Hot work, such as welding and flame cutting, poses a significant fire hazard in industrial operations due to the production of sparks.

Spark production during cutting is particularly hazardous as they are more abundant and can travel longer distances. When combined with flammable vapors, sparks can immediately ignite fires. Hidden smoldering fires can also flare up later when no one is present. It is crucial to closely supervise hot work conducted by outside contractors, as approximately one-third of cutting and welding fires occur during their operations.

To address these risks, established standards be followed mandating the development of fire prevention and protection plans for hot work conducted outside designated hot-work areas. One requirement is to have a fire-watch person present whenever hot work is performed in a location where a significant fire could develop or certain conditions exist. These conditions include:

- Combustible materials located within 35 feet of the hot work, or more than 35 feet away if they can easily be ignited by sparks.
- Openings in walls or floors within a 35-foot radius.
- Exposed combustible materials in adjacent spaces, including concealed spaces like wall cavities or spaces beneath floors.
- Combustible materials located on the opposite side of metal partitions, walls, ceilings, or roofs from the hot work area, which can be ignited by conduction or radiation.

A hot-work permit program should be implemented, requiring a permit for all hot work conducted on or near a covered process, including permanent locations. The permit should contain essential information such as the date, work to be performed, location, available firefighting equipment, assigned fire watch, pre-work area inspection, and authorized signatures.

The designated fire watch must have fire-extinguishing equipment readily available and be trained in its usage. They should also be familiar with the operation of fire alarms and be vigilant for fires in exposed areas. In the event of a fire, the fire watch should attempt to extinguish it within the available equipment's capacity or raise the alarm. The fire watch should be maintained for at least 30 minutes after completing hot work to detect and extinguish any smoldering fires.

Before commencing hot work, additional precautions should be taken, including:

- Preventing sparks or molten metal from passing through doorways, cracks, or holes in walls and floors.
- Moving all exposed combustible materials at least 50 feet away from cutting and welding operations. If adequate separation cannot be achieved, noncombustible curtains must be used.
- Sweeping floors clean and wetting down or covering wooden floors with noncombustible fire blankets.

By adhering to these safety measures, the risks associated with hot work can be minimized, reducing the likelihood of fire incidents in industrial settings.

* 9 7 9 8 3 9 7 4 1 5 4 8 4 *